Journey Across the Smiles

Journey Across

the Smiles

Recognizing

Your Choice

to

FEEL GREAT EVERY DAY

Judi Ronco

Judi Ronco

Dedication

First, I am dedicating this book to all the beautiful people I interacted with along my three-year journey across the country. Because of your willingness to open your hearts and share your dreams, joys, and struggles, this book exists. Each of you began as a stranger and with your delightful stories of seeing the good in your life, you became more like family, touching my life in amazing ways. I am a better person for having spent precious moments with each of you. Thank you.

In addition, I am dedicating this book to all of you whom I haven't met, who have dreams of a more fulfilling life and want to know what you can do to assist those dreams in coming to fruition. This book was written with great love and joy knowing that the simple act of feeling good, being happy right here and now, offers a tremendous benefit to you. Can a person want more and still be satisfied with what they already have? Absolutely! In fact, that's the key! Appreciating where you are and what you have in any moment opens doors that welcome into your experience the magic you seek, all that you desire. By the time you finish reading this book, you will be well on your way to recognizing the benefits of feeling good, feeling grateful, and what that means to each moment of your life, this day, and all those to come.

This understanding is aptly expressed by Marie Howe from *What the Living Do*:

"We want the spring to come and the winter to pass. We want whoever to call or not to call, a letter, a kiss – we want more and more then more of it. But there are moments, walking, when I catch a glimpse of myself in the window glass, say, the window of the corner video store, and I'm gripped by a cherishing so deep for my own blowing hair, chapped face, and unbuttoned coat that I am speechless:

I am living…"

"When you arise in the morning,

think of what a precious privilege it is

to be alive —

to breathe,

to think,

to enjoy,

to love."

- Marcus Aurelius

Contents

Welcome

In April of 2014, I made a huge decision in my life. I sold most of my worldly possessions and went on the road in a 19-foot conversion van that I called Van-Go. Inspirational quotes decorated the outside of the van that became my home for the next several years. It took me on a journey I could never have imagined, far more impactful than the original plan to visit waterfalls! As I traveled across forty of the fifty United States, the smiles, tears, hugs, and stories of the strangers I met enriched my life in more ways than the amazing sights I saw ever could.

Fifteen years earlier, I stopped reading, watching, or listening to the news because of my aversion to the melodrama. It occurred to me that good news felt better and must be much easier to find. So, in addition to my waterfall agenda, I decided I would report happy news from across the nation as I traveled. I set out to meet as many people as possible and ask them to share something good happening in their lives. My intention was to compensate in some small way for the negative outpouring of the media! What an adventure it turned out to be. I had already set up a travel blog where I described the places I visited including pictures and personal insights. It seemed easy enough to add a happy news section and call it Bright Spots. In preparing to write this book, I revisited those Bright Spots and they felt more like waves of light flowing in, around, and through me. They will be woven throughout the upcoming pages like a tapestry that we are all such an integral part of.

Start from the very beginning and take your time reading through the entire book. That will be the most delightful way to participate in the adventure. It will also allow you to feel your presence beside me, giving you more of a sense of being there. Later, it might be fun to go back and reread your favorites! My intentions are that:

1 - You enjoy the stories and are entertained by them.
2 - You resonate with at least one story on some level.
3 - You choose to find your own Bright Spot each day.
4 - You begin to crave the significant benefits of feeling good.
5 - You recognize the power YOU have to shift your thoughts in any given moment.

Feeling good is the most important thing you can offer to your personal well-being. The quality of your life and those around you also benefit. I want to feel good far more often than not, and so do you! How effortless it can be to discover a reason to feel good will become clear to you as you read. I discovered that every single person I asked had something to tell me. Some were less enthusiastic than others but shared nonetheless. Telling me about a moment, a past event, or a dream they cherished made both of us feel good. With each step, in each face, I saw a part of myself. I felt into the hearts of infants, seniors, and ages between. The similarities among races, ethnicities, economic levels, and walks of life were astounding. They brought me closer to each person and to myself. Verbal comments as well as emails from the precious people I interacted with helped me realize how much fun it was to consistently find the "golden nugget" in each day. Also, the good news I shared with them reignited a sense of gratitude and effervescence in my life.

Take a leap, be curious, read on, and decide to make the most of your magnificent life by joining me and the many strangers I had the pleasure of interacting with. Learn to recognize the "gem," the Bright Spot, in every one of your days. Allow your life to become a bold and beautiful celebration of joy!

Be open! Be aware! Be transformed! Be empowered! Be happy! BE YOU!

Fabulous Free Gifts

Journey Across the Smiles

Since the overarching theme of the book is about feeling good, I'm offering you a list of 33 song titles from my personal cross-country playlist. After submitting your email address on my website, check your inbox for this FREE gift! Check them out on YouTube or wherever you get your music! They will be sure to entertain you, inspire you, and make you smile. You might even laugh out loud. Below are the first five selections.

1 - Feeling Good by Michael Bublé
2 - Raise Me Up by Josh Groban
3 - I Believe by Elvis Presley or Frankie Laine
4 - It's a Great Day to Be Alive by Travis Tritt
5 - It's a Wonderful World by Louis Armstrong

In addition, once you sign up on my website, you will periodically receive additional feel-good stories, Q&As from my workshops, and inspirational messages all of which will prompt you to allow a little more sunshine into your life.

judironco.com

Thanks again! Read on and enjoy the Journey Across the Smiles.

Benefits to You, the Reader

You will reap numerous benefits from reading this book and imbibing its messages. These benefits are ones that I have personally experienced. There are likely to be many others. Listed below are just a few:

What you can expect from recognizing the good news in each day:
- more positive energy
- clearer perspective
- less stress
- more frequent smiles
- confidence in having successful days
- higher self-esteem/self-worth
- harmony in your life

What you can expect from recognizing your connection to others:
- feelings of community
- potential support system
- sense of belonging
- greater sense of well-being
- desire to spend time with friends
- encouragement to meet new people
- increased feelings of happiness

What you can expect from feeling and expressing gratitude:
- improved relationships
- enhanced long-term joy/optimism
- clarity and power to choose how you view your world
- increased ability to pass through challenges more easily
- acknowledgement of your growth potential if you make a mistake
- less frequent criticism of yourself/increased self-esteem
- improved health

As a life coach, while I was researching a list of positive emotions for a client, I came across an article written about a speech given at a Stanford University event. The contents support my experiences and overall purpose of this book, giving additional credence to the immense benefits of feeling great for even a brief period *each day*. It seemed pertinent to share it with you.

The following passages are from an article posted on Be Well Stanford regarding the talk given by Barbara Frederickson, PhD on May 12, 2016, at the Stanford Health Promotion Network's Summit VI: Crafting Your Culture. Dr. Frederickson received her post doctorate degree at UC Berkley. Her interest in this field began when she was a graduate student in the early 1990's. The article, in its entirety, can be found at bewell.stanford.edu/the-power-of-positive-emotions/

"The power of positive emotions – Experiencing positive emotions is more than just 'a nice feeling.'"

Day to day experiences of positive emotions add up to make our physical hearts healthier and more resilient. Sharing a smile or laugh with another may be providing a mini tune-up for our cardiovascular systems. Think of people you spent time with during the day. Did you feel close or in tune with them? Reflecting on human interaction/connection raises our emotional well-being.

The gap between the science of psychology and the value of studying human emotions has been narrowing over the last several decades. It started with research on the effects of negative emotions and has more recently shifted to an interest on the positive emotions and their effect on our physical well-being. Positive emotions serve a similar purpose as sources of nourishment. Science is now showing that experiencing happiness, contentment, gratitude, and a host of other positive feelings influence how our brains work. Our mindsets are broadened thus becoming more flexible.

The more frequently we engage with such positive emotions on a consistent basis for even the slightest period of time, their value accumulates to help us create superior versions of who we currently are. Dr. Frederickson called this the "broaden-and-build theory of positive emotions."

Judi Ronco

Section 1 – The Adventure Before THE Adventure

Have you ever had the experience of deciding to change something pretty big in your life? Thinking, *this…is…IT!* You thought it out, made the necessary plans, acted, and were quite content with your new – whatever it was. You went along with your big decision, and things were going pretty great. THEN, one day, you realized that something different had occurred to you, providing an even more tremendous appeal and the process began all over again. You wonder why you're no longer content with your first big decision. There was nothing you necessarily wanted to get away from. It wasn't that you doubted that the first decision was a good one. None of that, you just felt compelled to try something new and different. It felt like a change that would bring you additional happiness, a new challenge, or simply a change of pace. You knew it was going to be a "biggie" but the urge was too strong to allow any potential trepidation to stop you! I bet just about everyone has experienced this at one time or another in their lives.

In this first section, I describe the first big change that I thought was "the one"! It served me quite well on many levels including physically, mentally, emotionally, and spiritually. I didn't make the new choice because I was unhappy or dissatisfied with the initial one. It just called to me in a highly charged way, as it was pretty far out of my already stretched comfort zone. It would turn out to be a chapter in my life that took me by storm and gave me a rainbow that would never fade.

Join me in my unprecedented choice!

Chapter 1 – A 2,000-Mile Move at Age 55

"Life is short, break the rules...and never regret anything
that makes you smile."

— MARK TWAIN

I had always heard it was the kids who moved away from home when they grew up, but not in my case. As a child and young adult, I did all the expected things: I achieved high grades in school, went to college, got married, raised children...you get the picture. Make no mistake, I loved every aspect of that part of my life, especially being a mother. It has to this day been one of my grandest "accomplishments" and sweetest joys. Teaching my three beautiful children to love and accept themselves unconditionally, to always follow their heart, and to be true to themselves, eventually got me to wondering if I were doing the same for myself. Was I being true to myself? In other areas, I sensed that something just wasn't connecting for me.

The first thing in my life that I questioned was where I was living. I didn't like the severe weather on the East Coast, especially the harsh winters and high level of humidity in the summer. With my kids grown and settled and me about to retire, I started to wonder if I could live somewhere else. The "why not?" I experienced brought me to making that first big change. I decided to move to New Mexico, nearly two-thousand miles away. I knew only one person there but that was good enough for me. It felt good. It felt right. And when I shared this plan with my children, they were as supportive as any mother could have hoped. I didn't know how long I'd stay or even if I'd like it there. I *did* know from a place deep within me that it was the best thing for me to do at that time. I asked my younger and only sister, Tanya, who was godmother to all my kids, to keep an eye on them in my physical absence and she accepted the opportunity with great love and commitment. For that, I'll always be grateful.

My move to New Mexico came on the heels of my retirement from teaching special needs children. I lived there for four amazing years. The things I chose to involve myself with while living in the Land of Enchantment also felt like outpourings of who I truly was. As a teacher, I had always wanted to teach subjects left out of traditional curriculum. So, in New Mexico, I started a youth group called High Vibes for a few chosen local kids. I helped them to recognize aspects of themselves that were strong, healthy, and joyful and how to nurture those attributes. I also got excited about a new hobby of altering women's clothing that had been hanging in their closets for years and lost their appeal. With a little redesign, I could transform the garment to represent more of who the women had become over the years: the same at their core, yet something adventurously different. It was great fun, and looking back, it was almost a metaphor for my own personal development. But the pastime that had the most significant influence on my next BIG choice (to be revealed in Chapter 2), was working a part-time job in a small international boutique in Old Town Albuquerque. Wares from Guatemala, Peru, and Ecuador lined the walls and filled the racks with colors of the rainbow. It was delicious. As a saleswoman, I had the pleasure of chatting with visitors from all over the globe. I heard stories from their travels, their hometowns, and the purpose of their journeys. Those brief encounters began to seep into my very soul. Over time, an increasingly noticeable itch was growing as quickly as daffodils in spring. I knew that another big decision was on the horizon.

The second major aspect of my life that I questioned was the religion I was indoctrinated with from birth. The beliefs held within it definitely did not resonate with the person I believed I was. It wasn't until my early forties that I began a spiritual path away from the dogma of the church and closer to my true nature. Through the spiritual practices that I learned, especially meditation and chanting; I came to realize the divinity within each of us. I began to show up in my life in a fresh way. I learned how to be still and honor the silence. I saw myself as well as others in a more compassionate and accepting way. I began to take more responsibility for my choices and I even began to feel more connected to everyone I knew. This new awareness definitely felt like it was a shift toward being truer to myself. To add to this new and wonderful perspective, when I moved to New Mexico, I had the distinct pleasure of becoming friends with several shamans. At that point, I didn't even know what a shaman was. After witnessing their respect for the earth, everything that inhabits it and their ability to interact with their own energy as well as other's in a loving and healing way, I embarked on a journey I couldn't have possibly imagined. I studied for several years to become a shaman myself. I learned to acknowledge and respect people's various paths in life as well as how to guide them, if they chose, to discover more about their own authentic selves and ways of living that were harmonious. My training as a shaman only enhanced my earlier shift toward a more spiritual lifestyle. The appreciation I felt for what I learned and who I was becoming continues to this day. I'm certain that my heightened sense of belonging contributed greatly to my BIG adventure that would follow years later and which this book is about.

It amazes me today as I look back, that so many people I had never seen before welcomed me so graciously, were more like me than unlike me in so many ways, and made me feel right at home. This gift that had unfolded before me was greatly responsible for my BIG adventure coming up next.

Chapter 2 – Dream Revealed

"It takes a lot of courage to show your dreams to someone else."

— ERMA BOMBECK

I've decided! I'm doing it! I'm really going to do it! I'm going to travel across the country seeking a grand adventure...by myself!

Was I crazy? Maybe just a tad, but that's what's always kept me going with a lighthearted, excited, curiosity about life. I was ready to tell my three grown children (Matthew, thirty-two, Rachel, twenty-six, and Nicole, twenty-five) that I was about to go on the road solo! I wondered how they were going to respond, especially since just a few years prior, I had hit them with my move to New Mexico!

I booked a flight from Albuquerque to Baltimore and let them know that I had some interesting news. I could hear their internal dialogue now, "Here she goes again." A new adventure was on the horizon for me! I'm sure that my decision was "right for me" because I got goose bumps all over when I thought about how it would feel to journey into the unknown. That happens to me frequently whenever my inner voice agrees with my outer choice.

Shortly after my arrival into BWI (Baltimore-Washington International) airport, we got together and I broke the news. "So, guys, your mother is planning to travel across the country to...see what she can see."

Three heads, like oscillating fans, rotated to each other in turn. Then came the questions.

> Q- When did you decide this? A- Recently, sort of.
> Q- Where exactly will you be traveling to? A- Not really sure yet.
> Q- How are you doing this? A- Probably some kind of RV.
> Q- How long do you think you'll be on the road? A- Have no idea.
> Q- Are you really going by yourself? A- Yep

The oscillating heads resumed until finally a consensus was expressed. Paraphrasing, of course, their two cents went something like this: Well, you moved two-thousand miles away after retirement to follow your dream. You taught us to follow our hearts all our lives. We can only offer you the same advice. Go for it. This was followed by Rachel's words of wisdom "make good choices." We all laughed.

I saw, at that point, by the look on my son's face, that he wasn't completely convinced that this was a good idea. He reminded me that neither geography nor navigation were strong qualities of mine. He created a travel blog for me with instructions to post regularly. I agreed. I do believe it was put in place so my kids wouldn't worry about me, and I loved it! Little did I know that it would be the platform I'd need to share the magnificent stories of the people I met along my travels.

Returning to my house in Albuquerque, I was consumed with discovering where all the waterfalls and national parks were in the United States. For weeks, my laptop was open and the U.S. wall map and push pins were ready for action. Then reality struck! How was I going to make this happen?

Breathe, Judi. I believe that once a person makes a strong commitment to do anything, the puzzle pieces will begin to fall into place! I went to an RV show to check out my options. Wow! There were some pretty large options in size and price. I decided not to think about it for a while. The following week, having lunch at a neighborhood café, I overheard someone mention the term "conversion van." That was a new term for me, so I did what any self-respecting woman requiring quality information would do; I Googled it. Up popped a dealership with one of those vehicles on their lot. I checked it out the following day.

At first, it seemed a bit small, but once I got inside, it felt doable. Not a week later, I found myself without a Toyota Corolla and the proud new owner of a 19-foot conversion van, whiter than snow! I imagined it having an ice cream truck horn, the kind I remember from my childhood. Great! Now I have a residence on wheels. What's next?

Chapter 3 – This Stuff Has Got to Go

"Life presents you with so many decisions. A lot of times they're right in front of your face and they're really difficult, but we must make them."

— BRITTANY MURPHY

My new vehicle had buttons, hoses, clamps, and cables that I have never seen before. *Oh man, I'm going to have to read that manual.*

It wasn't long before it occurred to me that I would need to downsize big time if I were going to live in that box! I was going from a full three-bedroom house to a 19-foot van…whoa! Where does a girl start to decide what to store if she ever lands again, what to let go of completely, and what she will need to survive on the road?

Preparing for this journey of living an entirely new lifestyle was going to be an amazing adventure in and of itself. I must admit, the sheer excitement of it all did not come without a modicum of angst. I felt compelled to list the topics I needed to consider.

    1 - What to store, get rid of, or squeeze into the van
    2 - Getting mail without an address
    3 - Grocery shopping strategies with a tiny fridge
    4 - Having to pay to do laundry
    5 - Internet and phone service accessibility
    6 - Gas usage and expense
    7 - Dumping my own spot-a-potty

This may seem like a lot to take on for someone not passionate about embarking on a wild journey of unforeseen events, but I'm loving every minute of it…okay, most minutes. As hectic as it had been and would be until I got on the road, I couldn't complain. I did have to keep reminding myself that a dream was coming true for me and the support of my family, friends, coworkers, and other RV-ers who had been there and done that had been a wonderful gift!

With the help of friends, I held multiple estate sales out of my garage. It was great to see that items I loved and served me well go to a new home to serve a new person or family. When all sales were complete, I realized I needed a ten by five storage unit to house my remaining possessions. I rented one on a month-to-month basis, filled it up, and then went to work stocking the van. I strategically found cabinets, drawers, cubbies, and pockets for what would now serve me in this tiny living space.

To get used to my new home, I spent several nights in the van in the driveway. I learned when to duck my head and where to put my pillow for reading support. Overall, navigation of my new space was becoming more familiar.

The day I planned to leave New Mexico, the place that had been my home for four years, to venture out into the unknown was quickly approaching...only three days to go. Still there was much more to learn...and solutions to the topics mentioned above. Somehow, I knew I would be ready when I needed to be!

Chapter 4 - Information Overload: I Got This!

"You can't calm the storm, so stop trying. What you can do is calm yourself. The storm will pass."

— TIMBER HAWKEYE

Garmin, folded paper maps, Google maps, WAZE, and the winner is... all of the above. Given my history of getting lost, I couldn't possibly have too many resources!

Those last few days before I headed out, I learned about boondocking. That's when you stop for the night without using the electricity, sewer, or water provided by the campground. Though that would rarely happen, I still needed to know how to hook everything up. I practiced hooking up the electric cables, water hoses, and sewer apparatus on one overnight stay at a nearby campground just to get my feet wet. I was quite impressed with myself. The morning brought rain, and the experience of getting drenched while unhooking everything and putting it back in its proper storage was a slightly different story. Not fun, but amusing. I really did get my feet wet...as well as the rest of me!

I discovered that the size of your vehicle mattered when it came to booking a reservation at a campground. Some sites require a certain length, often much longer than my van. Some campgrounds only allow recreation vehicles that are 'self-contained' meaning they have a shower and heat and air conditioning...none of which I had in my van. I almost became concerned until I discovered PASSPORT AMERICA, an organization that has researched hundreds of campgrounds all over the country for details that matter to travelers looking for overnight lodging. It was a great find and served me well throughout my entire adventure.

I was feeling more comfortable about the interior size of the van after a few nights' practice, but still feeling some trepidation about the long haul. Interestingly enough, as the universe would have it, the day before "take-off," a friend invited me to explore one last wonder of New Mexico...Carlsbad Caverns. First thing in the morning, we'd be off on a mini adventure. Of course, I drove the van for additional practice.

Chapter 5 – Carlsbad Caverns: A Claustrophobia Scare

"Courage is the first of all human qualities because it's the quality which guarantees all others."

— WINSTON CHURCHILL

My throat thickened, my stomach tightened, and my knees weakened! Switchbacks (sharp U-turns along a path) at 750 feet beneath the earth's surface...I didn't know if I could do it! How much did seeing the proclaimed wonder of the Carlsbad Caverns really mean to me?

"You'll be fine, honest. It'll be worth it, I promise," my friend Marie repeated over and over as I stood nearly breathless at the entrance to the cave. I was feeling intimidated by the thought of going on a group tour. What if I freaked out? I'd be so embarrassed.

I walked away for a little while and reminded myself that I knew how to deal with prickly, panicky feelings. I closed my eyes and took several slow deep breaths. After a few rounds, I could still feel the heightened palpitation of my own heart, but it was lessening with each breath. As my heart rate returned to some semblance of comfort, a moment came when I realized I wanted to overcome my fear more than to actually experience the cavern. It became a personal mission rather than simply a sightseeing excursion.

My friend smiled as she saw me approach the low hanging entrance, shaped like a teardrop lying on its side, white-knuckling the handrail to my right.

"Let's do it," I declared.

One step at a time, I glided along the rocky floor. I guess I figured if I didn't actually lift my feet up, I had a better chance of getting through in one piece. Way down inside of me, I felt a chuckle reacting to my thought. Along with that brief chuckle, a great deal of internal dialogue was going on while I was walking through the rooms in the caverns, marveling at the immensity of the rock formations, the wonderment of the "bottomless" pool, the unexpected splendor of the spot where a stalactite (a formation attached to the roof of the cave) and a stalagmite (a formation attached to the floor of the cave) were almost touching. That formation was referred to as the Eternal Kiss. There seemed to be a soft utterance of the miracle of it all.

No one noticed the tears flowing gently down my cheeks. Had I missed this magical underground world; it would have been a tremendous loss. Self-adjustment is powerful. I was grateful for the reminder to breathe my way into a calm state, allowing me to face my fear...a fear that was unfounded. Most of them are, I suppose.

I was looking forward to the big day with each deep breath I took...one step closer to going on the road...on my own...across the country! Woohoo!

Chapter 6 – Maiden Voyage and the Birth of Bright Spots

A minute to reflect on my state of mind at that point. Words cannot accurately describe how I was feeling. Maybe ecstatic, hopeful, delirious, joyous, anxious, curious, and grateful would be a few samples that pale in comparison to what was stirring within me. I couldn't help but wonder if and when embarking on this magnificent journey would cease to seem surreal. I was fixin' to find out.

My first cross-country expedition took me from Albuquerque, New Mexico to Manhattan, New York. It was scheduled to take about nine days. My daughter Rachel and her wife Megan were arriving back to the states after a seven-day cruise and I offered to pick them up. What was I thinking? Maneuvering a 19-foot van in Manhattan at the "hustling, bustling, no regard for lanes or lights" cruise terminal was exactly like one might imagine. Nuts! I hid my panic well as the girls waved with sheer joy when they spotted me, so happy to see me. My smile, in return, was one more of relief for having survived getting in there in one piece. Arranging the details for that trip reminded me of the long-range planning required at the onset of each quarter when I was teaching. I always found it exhilarating to consciously choose your foreseeable future with all the "nooks and crannies" yet being ready to shift gears in an instant if life called for it! Thank goodness I didn't need to shift too many gears.

The first few days on the road again alone after I dropped the girls back home were packed with heart-thumping excitement. Other travelers and locals were curious about my "ice cream truck" story. Ways to relieve my van of that misconception were stirring in my mind! Would I get it painted with a fabulous design or completely change its color? Well, that would have to wait awhile. I was far more intrigued by the people I was meeting. Each time I shared a little about my intended adventure, I noticed people not only listened intently, but seemed to want to share something about themselves. It was wonderful to interact so easefully with perfect strangers, similar to when I first moved to New Mexico. I even got a few great tips from fellow full-timers.

18

Hungry and tired after a three-hour drive, I stopped at the Caravan Xpress Grill, a sports bar near Tucumcari, New Mexico. My palate was satisfied with a great burger, fries, and an iced tea. My feelings about the negative news breaks between sports action were less than comforting! I had decided a couple decades ago to stop watching the news and reading the newspaper…too much disturbing input for my taste. My boycott had been successful because I usually had a choice of what to expose myself to in regard to the media. Today, not so much. I found myself wishing the sports would hurry and return, even though I'm also not a huge sports fan. I shifted my focus to imaginings of what was next on my journey. In spite of the temporary annoyance, I was soon on the road again with a happy tummy and rested eyes, legs, and back.

While driving, I was reminiscing about the fun anecdotes of the people I had encountered so far. Tidbits of their positive adventures were shared with me, someone they didn't even know, and it made me smile. I had an epiphany…if those few folks were willing to share some goodness in their lives, I bet there would be many others willing to do the same. At that moment, I decided to broadcast good news from across the nation as part of my blog posts. How much fun would that be? I couldn't wait to try it out.

At the campground I reserved for the night, I noticed several enormous rigs, making my van look like a thumbnail! Dutch and Sherri, seventeen-year veterans at full-timing, came by to welcome me. Their huge Ford E350 truck was toting a forty-one-foot RV with three pull-outs *and* a ten-foot garage attached containing their two motorcycles! Wow! I bet they don't make many U-turns! We chatted a few minutes and when I got back to my van, I saw my sofa was elevated. I pulled it up only to find that my water tank was bulging! I quickly turned off the valve that allowed site water to come in. Then I went to the source and unscrewed the hose and got drenched…I forgot to turn the spigot off…rookie move for sure! With flashlight in hand, I made a mad dash for the office and the wonderful security man followed me back to the scene of the near disaster, showed me what I did wrong and released a good amount of water from the tank! The gadget I thought was the water pressure gauge was nothing more than a filter! He saved me. Blowing up my water tank within the first ten days out would have put a real "damper" on my upcoming plans.

After all that drama, I was ready for some grub! Just outside the campground was a diner called Rockin' Y's Roadhouse. I walked over and ordered a fabulous salad. There, I discovered my first bit of traveling good news. One of the owners of the restaurant was waitressing. She said I looked exhausted, so I briefly explained that I just got into town, almost blew up my water tank, and had only been on the road a little over a week. I told her how the man who offered to help me out was a real bright spot in my day. She chuckled compassionately. I took this opportunity to tell her about my "mission." She was more than happy to oblige. When she brought my salad, she sat down to chat. She told me she also worked at Mesalands Community College, right there in Tucumcari, and was extremely proud about it. She explained that, in addition to offering fully accredited academic programs enabling students to earn a wide variety of degrees and certifications, it is also home to the North American Wind Research and Training Center. She was especially excited that the college had a world class wind energy technology, was the only community college in the nation with its own turbine, and had a bronze foundry. Additional fun facts about Mesalands Community College were that it was the only one that allowed Freshmen and Sophomores to do their own digging and that their campus included a Dinosaur Museum housing all student-found bones! Her face was aglow throughout her delightful sharing. What a lovely dinner bonus. Almost like dessert! I thanked her and double-checked to make sure she didn't mind if I posted her story on my travel blog.

I walked back to the campground, climbed up into my van and pulled out my laptop to post the day's happenings. As I recalled the helpful security man and the woman in the restaurant, I got a brilliant idea. Any feel-good stories from anyone who wanted to share would now be called BRIGHT SPOTS on my blog! And, so it was!

For the most part, I invited the people that you'll be reading about to share their feel-good stories about their lives with me. I want to mention that here because I haven't been specific in most stories about how some of the conversations got started. I did share my mission to gather peoples' good news in every case, but it would be redundant to repeat that in each story. On a few occasions, the person decided to share without me prompting them. In those stories, I do mention that.

Have fun and feel good as you read the delightful stories ahead.

Judi Ronco

Did you know...?

There are 86,400 seconds

in each day.

How many

will you choose

to feel good about?

There is always value in the present moment. Look for it.

Simply recognizing the uniqueness of the moment
is beneficial.

Judi Ronco

Section 2 – THE Adventure: Bright Spots Galore!

This section is a compilation of many of the remarkable experiences I had throughout my personal journey. I learned to value the choice to feel good as often as possible. On some occasions, I figured it out myself. Other times, I was reminded by an incredible group of individuals who were willing to share with me their stories of great things, big and small, happening in their lives. My personal interaction with each of the people you will read about has brightened my life in so many ways. I'll mention a few of the ways here so that you may get a taste of what's to come.

We are all more alike than we are different. Feeling good is a choice that makes all the difference in the quality of your life. We have so many things to feel good about. It's important to notice what you are focusing on. We have the power to shift our thoughts in any given moment.

I could go on and on, but I'll give you the opportunity to glean from these delightful and heartfelt stories what resonates with you.

Nine themes are depicted as chapters in Section 2 and each consists of several related Bright Spots of my family of strangers. You will discover in the nine chapters, adventures of mine and experiences of strangers that are the reason I was inspired to write this book. Recognizing the good in any situation and feeling appreciation for it adds unquestionable and remarkable value to life. Imagine finding a shiny penny at your feet, spotting a rainbow after a storm, holding a newborn, finishing a project, getting a return on your taxes, or remembering a special moment during your last vacation. How would you feel? If these events don't seem like big deals to you, I urge you to reconsider or find one of your own every single day. The tiniest, seemingly insignificant happy thought is what can make it all worthwhile and add immeasurable joy to your life.

Oftentimes, just one single thought can cause a shift that changes everything right then and there. In the movie *HOOK,* Peter Pan is urged to find his happy thought, which was his kids. That one thought enabled him to fly! Sometimes, the one single thought is the impetus for a domino effect of additional good-feeling thoughts that will make the positive difference. One scenario might be: You got a flat tire in the rain with no roadside assistance plan. You're bummed out. You become aware that you're definitely not feeling happy, and you don't like it. A single thought rises up: *Well, at least I have a spare.* Still not feeling all that good. Another thought arises: *At least it's daylight*, then another, *Glad I'm strong enough to change this darn thing*, then another, *Oh, well, I was only on my way home from work, so it won't cause me to be late.* OKAY, now you're feeling a lot better and have discovered several things to be grateful for despite the inconvenient situation.

Too often, we focus on the hassles or challenges of our day and go to bed feeling exhausted. It's difficult to look forward to yet another such day tomorrow. There's an old saying, "Seek and you shall find." If you take a moment during your day to find any feel-good thought, I assure you it will not have been in vain. We all have goodness in our lives; sometimes we forget to notice. Welcome the opportunity of seeking out yours. Enjoy!

Chapter 1 – Matters of Perspective

Love at the Laundromat

Never did I think I would be so happy to see an open laundromat at 7:00 in the morning. There was no such facility at the campground, the sky was cloud-covered with no break in sight, and I needed to get my grubby hiking, biking, climbing attire cleaned and ready for my next adventure. Things were mighty bleak until I saw the neon sign... "OPEN."

Having gathered all necessary supplies, I barreled through the opened front doors and plopped my sack on the counter. I walked over to the string of machines with a look that must have screamed HELP to the attendant on duty. A tall woman with broad shoulders, wide hips, and a sculpted face came from behind the high counter, sauntering to my aid.

"Is there something I can help you with, miss?" Her tone suggested that she was hoping I'd say, "No, thanks." Unfortunately, "Yes" was my only true answer. It had been decades since I needed a laundry facility outside my own residence. She sighed and took me through the procedure. I thanked her and she returned to her perch.

As I sorted and stuffed my clothes into the washing machines, I peeked over at the woman slouched over in her chair as if in possible discomfort. I wondered about her. Maybe she was lonely there. Maybe she had been there all night and was very tired. I couldn't help but think maybe a chat would help. I knew that often a slight distraction could make a world of difference in your day. I walked over with a smile as big as I could muster and thanked her again for her assistance. She didn't even look up. Undeterred, I rambled on about my adventure and what a rookie I still was at living on the road full-time. Nothing. Then I explained how glad I was that my campground didn't provide this amenity because it gave me the chance to meet her. She looked at me with a puzzled expression, furrowed brow, and all. I mentioned that meeting new people was one of my favorite aspects of traveling, and now she was part of my enjoyable experience.

She offered no response so I went back to wait for the wash cycle to end, all the while anticipating my next "move." Unexpectedly, she walked past my bench opening and closing several machine doors. Well, in my mind, that was a blatant invitation to engage her in conversation. I jumped all over it. I told her I was traveling and asking people I met to share something good going on in their lives.

Immediately, she retorted, "No sense in asking me. I work in here day in and day out. My only break is between midnight and 5:00 a.m. when I close up and get some shut-eye. Nothing good about that!"

I allowed a brief silence, noticing that she still stood before me. "Maybe there's something outside of here that makes you feel good?"

"Well, I can tell you one thing that doesn't thrill me. My daughter is a drug addict in no condition to take care of her own son! He's been living with me for nearly a year, and I'm too damn old to deal with his raging hormones." She took a deep breath and went on about how he doesn't want to listen, do homework, obey curfews, and so on. "Sorry I can't help with your little project, miss." She turned and walked away. I let it go.

I switched my wet clothes to the dryer. As I gazed at the swirling bumping motion of fabric through the slightly foggy door window, it occurred to me how similar this process was to us, people.

We bump and swirl and bang into things in our lives, then given enough time, through choice or by default, we come out of the experience softer, warmer, and nearly "wrinkle-free." I walked boldly right up to the woman and politely told her that I would be staying in the laundromat until she was able to share at least one tiny thing in her life that felt good and made her smile.

Her eyes widened and her mouth opened but nothing came out.

I smiled. "I'll be sitting on the longer bench reading. I have no other plans for today."

About thirty minutes passed by before she scurried over to where I sat and said, "I don't know what makes you think there is anything, miss. I hate to see you waste your day like this."

"Tell me more about your grandson, please. How old is he? What's his name? Is he involved in any sports? Is there a favorite dish he likes you to make him?"

That got her going! "Mostly he is a good kid, I guess. It ain't his fault he had poor raising until last year. He's only sixteen. I mean how much could the kid know about not making your grandma crazy? He loves my rice and beans, but I think his favorite might be my mama's recipe for grown-up mac n' cheese with bacon. Boy, can that kid eat a lot..."

I sat in awe, taking in every word. With every slight shift in her voice, her arms relaxed by her side, and her face lost half its wrinkles as she spoke, giving me the gift of unabashed pleasure! She even sat down.

"But he's pretty funny too. He gets me to laughing over things I never thought were funny, but when *he* tells me, they seem funny. And he's done a little better in school this semester. He's getting more homework done, too. When he asks me for help with his arithmetic, I tell him I have no idea what he's talking about. That makes us both laugh because he calls me his 'old-school' granny." She sat up tall and sighed.

I took this opportunity to chime in and ask, "Do you think you've learned anything from him since he moved in?"

She looked at me, out the window, at the clock, then back at me. "Life just doesn't have to be all that serious. You gotta let yourself laugh, even at yourself sometimes, ya know? I guess I need to think of him on these long boring days. I would probably feel better."

Then I asked if he has learned anything from her. She laughed hard and loud and stood up cinching her waist with her hands slightly above her hips, "You bet he has. I'm no pushover. That's for sure!"

I stood up too, scooping up my sack of clean laundry, and said, "Next time someone asks what's good in your life…" She looked at me with a tear in her eye and whispered, "Thank you" as she hugged me and my laundry and told me to have a good day.

I smiled and replied, "I already am." As I put my clothes in the van, I noticed the sun was shining.

A Mixed Bag in South Haven

Great news about Van-Go first thing in the morning was welcomed. The glowing engine light I noticed several days prior was only because of a loose gas cap! Whew! Woo-hoo!

As I strolled along the promenade at South Haven, Michigan, I passed by two incredible wall murals. One depicted the harbor with boats, seagulls, soaring kites, folks strolling along with ice cream and children riding their bicycles. The other mural depicted some historical aspects of the area. Peoples' talent never fails to amaze me and with my full-time traveling, I've been blessed to see a variety of creative genius.

I also had the pleasure of taking a picture of a darling elderly couple whose 50th anniversary was that day. They were so appreciative of my offer. I asked them what their secret was for having a long run marriage like theirs.

The woman explained, "There's no marriage quite like ours to begin with, and our secret isn't as profound as you might think. We decided to stay in love; that's all." She had a twinkle in her eye. Her husband winked at her and kissed her on her forehead. It was all I could do to keep a dry eye. How sweet they were!

On my way toward the shops, I heard a great deal of screaming. I turned and "what to my wondering eyes should appear, but a boat full of middle schoolers for all to hear!" That brought back memories of my teaching days. Ages eleven, twelve, and thirteen are so great and so loud!

After leaving South Haven, I stopped at a neighborhood grocery store to pick up a few things. Returning to the campground should have taken twenty-five minutes but took an hour and a half! It's amazing how one wrong turn can lead you to places so unfamiliar that you're not sure you will ever see anything you recognize again. I was so annoyed at myself. What a waste of time. At one point, I had to pull over and just breathe and breathe some more. I had not

31

been that ticked off in quite a while. I was not a "happy camper." I knew I had to snap out of the funk I was in or I would never find my way back.

I sat for about fifteen minutes waiting for some relief. I looked out the window and feelings of gratitude began to arise. It wasn't raining or dark and all four of my tires were inflated. I glanced down and saw my gas tank was near full. That was really good. I pulled out my trusty, old-school paper map with a million folds in it and calmly managed to find where I slipped up and how to get back on track. I continued to wonder how on earth I managed to make that wrong turn. Aah, perhaps a loud favorite song on my radio that beckoned to be sung, windows down, and a little driver's seat "dancing" might have done it! I missed the turn because I was having fun. How bad was that? No harm, no foul. Back before dark and dinner that never tasted so good, I had to laugh at myself.

Salesman Sees Past the Theft

My last stop in Maryland before I headed north was to have my van and scooter checked out for the long haul. I arrived at the dealership where Navid, the owner, greeted me with a smile as usual. Something immediately caught my attention. A scooter was sitting in the showroom with kids' handprints all over it. He explained that his business was part of a fundraiser last weekend for needy kids. He donated a small scooter to be auctioned off. One hundred percent of the proceeds went for the kids' needs. He invited several of the children to come to his shop and decorate the scooter with their handprints in various colors of paint. It was awesome. What a cool idea and generous offer.

He took my scooter to the service area along with the scooter "trunk" I purchased so it could be installed. There were no other customers, so we sat out front hanging out with his adorable six-month-old puppy. Navid, though pleasant, helpful, and efficient, didn't quite seem like himself. His eyes were not as bright, his movements were slightly labored, and his voice was melancholy. Nothing drastic, just different than I was used to. Since I purchased my scooter from Navid, I had been in his showroom on several occasions and had grown accustomed to his cheerful disposition and lighthearted manner. His energy felt heavy that day.

After a brief pause in our conversation, I asked how his morning had been. He looked at me quizzically and began to explain what had happened. Walking down his driveway toward his car, he noticed it had been broken into. The glove box door was ripped off and the locked zipper bag with last week's deposit was missing. He went on to tell me that he usually kept his checkbook and passport in the glove box as well, but the night before, he took those two items out because of an upcoming vacation he was planning.

"You know, I was upset about the money being gone, and after brooding about it for several hours, I stopped my rampage. It was so fortuitous that my checkbook and passport were not part of the theft, and I felt so grateful. They would have been much more difficult to replace, especially my passport. I guess I'll just have to sell a couple extra bikes this week!" He smiled the kind of smile I was accustomed to seeing.

I think sometimes you just have to find the nectar in an otherwise lousy situation! Navid did that and with a smile! He was surely an inspiration for me as I was preparing to take a long journey into unknown territory. I told him I would carry his beautiful outlook with me on my trip. We both smiled. By then, my scooter with its new trunk was hitched on the front rack of my van. I paid for his services and rode off feeling awestruck by the way he chose to see *his* experience while looking forward to *my* next one!

Mani-Pedi with a Twist

You never know what you'll experience in a nail salon. I was treating myself to a day of luxury with a massage and a nail makeover. When I slid my toes and fingers under the heat light to allow the polish to dry, the woman to my left spontaneously started up a conversation with me. Her name was Jan. She had been out of work for eight months and her unemployment was about to run out. Jan was going to lose her apartment. When she told me that, I half expected to be the recipient of a serious "pity party." Instead, to my delight, she smiled broadly and said that she was so grateful that her son offered to have her come stay with him. Then she talked to her friend on the phone about her situation and got a tip about an interesting job opening. The best part was when she laughed loudly and said, "Guess what else? I have an interview for that very position this afternoon, hence the mani-pedi!"

I was thrilled for her and I had a strong feeling that she would do fine at the interview. I told her that with a positive attitude like hers, she was likely to do well. Hoping she wouldn't mind letting me know later how the interview went, I handed her my card. She snatched my card up and said, "You bet I will and thanks."

It was over a week before I heard from Jan. I answered the phone, hearing sounds of excitement and loud background noise. Her words still came through clearly, "I DID IT. I got the job, Judi! I had to move to East Peoria this past weekend and I'm having dinner with my son and we're celebrating at a new restaurant near my new apartment. I'm having a blast unpacking and figuring out where every little thing will go. It's like a fresh start, a new beginning. Thanks for cheering me on last week. I so enjoyed meeting you and I know many others will, too. I hope your travels are wonderful and safe."

I couldn't get a word in. She was so ecstatic. Finally, I told her what an inspiration she was and how glad I was that she remembered to contact me. I wished her all the good fortune she deserved, including more mani-pedis on a regular basis. We both laughed.

Jan was able to find the good in a situation that others may have become depressed over. I believe that her positive outlook caused more good things to come to her. What a powerful gift we all possess to choose "I know there's a gem in this mess" perspective. I felt honored to share in a small slice of Jan's ever-expanding joyful life.

Amusing Reality Check

Driving into Pensacola, Florida, there were enormous fields of cotton. Beyond the few rows framing the roadside were bright strips of pure white as far as my eyes could see. It was a spectacular sight.

It had been a long day and arriving at a campground at night was never ideal. Fortunately, Wendell, the owner, took me to my site. He guided me in because it wasn't a pull-through. I had to back Van-Go into my spot with only the light of Wendell's flashlight. He told me to bundle up because it was going to be a chilly one. *Bundle up? This is Florida, for goodness sake! And it's only mid-November anyway. Really?!* Well, Wendell was spot on! Three blankets, two cups of tea, and a funny movie later, I was finally tired and warm enough to fall asleep.

The next morning was lovely. I walked around after breakfast with a light sweater and was quite comfy. For the most part, that particular RV Park was just that, a place to park your RV, no frills! The good news was that the owner's home was situated on a darling little pond and patrons were invited to share in its sweetness. Of course, where there's water, there's ME! Despite the lack of ambiance everywhere else on the "lot," that area around the pond compensated for it with its fragrant flowers and huge hundred-year-old trees. It was akin to being in an antique furniture shop. The old-wood aroma wafted across the air right past my nose. The trees were massive and barely holding onto their moss green, rust, crimson, and deep yellow leaves. Those giants offered the perfect back support. They provided shade for reading a great book. Listening to the frogs croaking incessantly as they jumped in and out of the pond was delightful. There were lily pads with large blossoms where dragonflies landed flapping their pearlescent wings. The entire day was a picture-perfect fall day with a crisp gentle breeze, and blue skies. The white fluffy clouds gliding by at varying speeds and shapes took me back to my childhood. Finding familiar shapes in the clouds used to take up an entire day back then.

Approximately 7:00 p.m. that evening, the weather went to hell in a handbasket! The skies lit up with the threat of thunderstorms. Some bolts felt like they reached from ground to sky, zig-zagging in all directions. Thunder followed, ranging from sharp loud cracks to long low rumbles.

Van-Go and I were "rocking and rolling" in response to the sudden gusts of wind. The owner, Wendell, even stopped at my van and asked if I would be okay with those winds. I told him in a somewhat sarcastic and strongly annoyed tone that I would find out shortly. The icing on the cake was his mentioning that there was a freeze warning broadcast for the middle of the night. Nice. My teeny tiny space heater and three blankets on top of me and my jeans and sweatshirt were just going to have to do!

Having survived the freaky night before, I got dressed with three layers of clothing under my coat. I was trying desperately to remember that I was in Florida, the Sunshine State. It was news to me that all of Florida wasn't created equal when it came to climate. The temperature at 8:46 a.m. the next morning was 31 degrees with a windchill of 26 and a high expected to be a whopping 45 degrees. Damn, I went to Florida to get *away* from the cold. I couldn't even take my scooter into town because of the cold. And to the beach, well....?! After I was done bellyaching, I opened my door, looked up and saw a flashing neon sign that read, "Come in and get warm." They didn't have to ask me twice. I walked across the street to a small coffee house and ordered a delicious cheese Danish. I warmed my hands by wrapping them around my cup of tea.

Feeling warm and cozy, I replayed my recent mind chatter consisting of one complaint after another and I didn't feel good at all. Pondering my less than pleasant attitude, I had to laugh at myself. I mean, really? There I was, on the adventure of a lifetime and I couldn't handle a little weather? At least I learned something valuable related to any joy I might feel for the remainder of my journey. This lifestyle not only requires a sense of adventure, but also a sense of HUMOR! With a half-eaten Danish in one hand and a cup of tea in the other, I decided to graciously accept that fact. With that being said, I also decided to set my sights on venues with warmer weather. After all, I had places to go, people to meet and a tan to revitalize!

Trading in a Rear-View Mirror Option

Glen Rose, Texas is home to Tres Rios Resort, a campground situated at the convergence of three rivers, good fishing, great walking paths, beautiful sunrises, and a wonderful restaurant. James was my Super Chef one evening. Fortunately for me, he was hired to prepare meals for the campers just over a month prior! With only a half dozen guests that night, during a lull after everyone was served, James happened by to check on me as he had with the other guests. Of course, I raved about the meal, and he shared a somewhat unexpected fact about himself.

"I wasn't always a cook. Actually, I was quite the wanderer, hopping trains and going as far as the cash I had on hand would get me. Then I'd do odd jobs and be on the rails again."

James' story was quite a long one. It was too long for our purposes here. The following highlights will suffice. At one point, he met the love of his life, got married, and settled down. After only a few years, his wife Michelle passed away. His first inclination was to go back to his old ways, seeing no point in staying around where everything reminded him of his unbearable grief. He admitted that he had been hit with a dose of mortality and decided life was too short to squander it away. So, he took several jobs cooking for small restaurants in Kansas. Cooking came easily for him. A few years later, he relocated to Glen Rose to apply for a maintenance position at the campground. During his interview they discovered he could COOK. He got hired on the spot as their chef and started taking over the kitchen the next day! He did a lot of thinking during his off hours and felt a whole new James almost erupting inside. He met his current wife, Cassie. He described her as his best friend and support system. I could see a light in his eyes resembling a young child on Christmas morning when he spoke her name. It made me smile. His expression softened a bit as he reflected on his sense of pride that his improved attitude was being nurtured by the woman he loved. The sincerity in his voice told me he was humbled as well as grateful to have Cassie by his side to support him as well as their dreams for the future.

As we continued to talk, he told me about his passion for music. He had played guitar with a few guys back in Kansas and still plays a couple times a month in a local pub in Texas. James plans to keep his guitar playing alive but just on the side. He started taking a course in certified dietary management (CDM). He found that he also had developed a passion for cooking and seeing the guests enjoy their meal. We laughed when he said that he figured both avenues, playing guitar and cooking, were related to entertaining. Before we parted ways, I expressed my delight in his newfound happiness and contentment. I asked him if he learned anything from those experiences. He was quick to say now that he felt so much joy moving forward, he would never look back. Words of wisdom for sure.

Happy Divorce?

Extraordinary artwork, fantastic food, and a surprising anecdote were waiting for me at the Indigo Palette on 4th Street in Sioux City, Iowa. I randomly chose this eclectic gallery and café to stop in for lunch strictly because of its name. I have done that frequently and was always delighted with my experience. "What's in the name?" some ask. For me, at least, there was definitely something in the name, "Indigo Palette." It sounded intriguing. The café walls were lined with a myriad of unusual art. On display were still-life oils, chalk designs, mixed media on metal sheets, and conglomerations of unrelated objects swaying from the ceiling. It kept my eyes busy while I waited for my server to take my order and again while waiting for my meal to arrive.

My server, Melanie, was also the barista. She greeted me with a huge smile as she approached my table. "What can I get for you this fine day?"

Now that's a happy waitress, I thought. I glanced at the menu again, having been sidetracked earlier by the ambiance, and ordered a Greek salad with a side of sweet potato fries! Melanie told me they had the best sweet potato fries in the city and if I didn't love them there would be no charge! "Oh, I'm sure I'll love them," I replied giggling. Melanie grinned from ear to ear and said my lunch would be there soon.

I couldn't help but wonder what it was that made her so cheerful. Did she really love her job that much? Was it her birthday? I knew that I was going to have to ask when she brought my food. In less than ten minutes, my food was delivered. The cold crisp salad and hot crunchy fries were perfect. "Go ahead and try one," Melanie urged. She waited with her hands on her hips as I picked up a sweet potato fry and blew on it gently to cool it. I bit into it and could feel a sigh coming on. It was, indeed, scrumptious! Without my uttering a word, she looked at me with a slight "I told you so" look in her eyes and said without hesitation, "I told you so!" We both laughed out loud.

Then to my surprise, before I had the opportunity to inquire about her wonderful mood, she sat down across from me and asked if I wanted to hear something really awesome. Of course, I did.

"I'm getting a divorce in a couple of weeks!"

I didn't quite know how to respond. Her glow and her news seemed like a mismatch. She went on to explain that she and her husband were best friends before they got married. They had such fun together being able to talk about anything under the sun. After being married for three years, they decided that it wasn't working for more reasons than she had time to share. It felt like they were strangers and all they did was argue. At first, this realization was devastating to both of them. They discussed marriage counseling, but that didn't pan out. It took much deliberation on their parts to finally conclude that a divorce was probably the best option. Melanie went on to tell me the craziest thing. Once they had decided to get divorced, the very idea of it was such a relief that they started getting along again like when they were dating! Until their divorce became final and all the papers were signed, they opted to be roommates with the understanding they may possibly continue to live together in their new roles as "buddies."

I stood up and hugged her. I wished her every happiness however she finds it and congratulated her for doing what was best for her and her "man" regardless of societal norms. Way to go, Melanie!

Hearing her story tickled me to no end. How great were these two individuals to be in touch with what their needs were, adjusting their life choices, and seeing their situation with fresh eyes! It's about being happy, after all!

Valentine's Day: An Obligation or A Celebration

I had an unexpected experience in a pharmacy while waiting for a prescription to be filled. Across the aisle, people packed the sizable sections devoted to Valentine's cards and gifts. Some were quite focused and others were scurrying like field mice. As I stood back and observed for a while, what I witnessed was very intriguing. I saw quite a range in age among the shoppers and more men than women. Some appeared to be doing their own shopping for cards, while others shopped for cards for their children to give to their classmates. None of that seemed out of the ordinary to me. Then I decided to start looking for cards and gifts so I could get an "insider's" look at what felt like a bit of a frenzy! I saw facial expressions that could be described as confused, desperate, excited, irritated, starry-eyed, joyful, etc. What I found to be unexpected were the "less than loving" expressions.

Then I heard one man say to another, "If I don't find her just the right card that says what she wants to hear, I'm screwed." Okay, definitely not what I expected.

So, I thought I would do a little experiment. I guess I'm lucky I didn't get asked to leave. I walked around until I found a face that beckoned for verbal release. I approached a young woman appearing possibly irritated and I asked, "Having trouble finding just the right card?" Her response was, "Yeah, I guess. It probably doesn't really matter what it says as long as I give him one. He's into all this crap." I just smiled.

I moved on and spotted an elderly gentleman, hands slightly shaking, reading away. I said, "It looks like you must have a sweetheart." He said, "Yep, I do, same one for fifty Valentine's Days this year." I commented that she probably really appreciated receiving his card every year. "Oh, she doesn't mind. She puts up with me and my cards." I asked him what he meant. "Well, she already *knows* I love her. I fall in love with her again every single day. I'm the one who likes to find her a card that says that a little different way every year. It's getting more challenging these days." I wanted to hug him, but instead I told him that I hope he finds what he is looking for and that his wife is a very fortunate woman. He smiled and said, "I'm the lucky one."

My prescription was ready, so I left with mixed emotions regarding this big-ticket holiday. I stopped at another store to pick up some groceries and once again the Valentine's Day card aisles were packed. People were clamoring about like shoppers near midnight Christmas Eve! Arms were wrapped around stuffed animals, and baskets were filled with mugs, flowers, candy...you name it.

I approached a very young man, maybe in his early twenties who was holding an enormous stuffed teddy bear and asked, "Wow, who's the lucky recipient of THAT?" He said with a troubled voice, "My girlfriend. Yeah, she pretty much told me that if I didn't get her something even better than last year, she'd be pissed." I just said that I was sure she would love it. I thought to myself, *how sad.*

I was not about to end my experiment with that interaction. I finally saw an older lady in the next aisle of cards, smiling away with quite a few cards in her grip. I asked if she wanted me to get her a basket. She said, "Thank you, but I'm almost done. Of course, if I have any *more* grandchildren, I'll start needing a basket!" I was so tickled with her. She was having a fabulous time picking out kiddy cards.

Before I left, I spoke to one final woman, maybe in her forties. She must have read every single card displayed. I was looking at cards too, so I commented, "Sometimes, it's hard to find one that's just right." She replied quickly, "I know! My husband and I got married on Valentine's Day and I never know whether to get him an anniversary card or a Valentine's card. I usually get him both, but this year, it's different." I asked why. She explained that after ten years of marriage, they split up for a few months in the summer. Now they were back together and it meant even more to her to tell him how much he really means to her. I stood there a few seconds then I suggested perhaps she could make a card herself so that she could say exactly what she felt. She looked at me with kind of a blank stare and then said, "Oh my gosh, I never thought of doing that. Thank you." Before I could say anything, she turned and walked away. I thought about that day for quite some time.

Whether to include this particular selection in the book was a decision that took some contemplation. I decided it ultimately contained great value regarding perspective on many levels, so in it went! You may notice that different perspectives induce different emotions. Some are feel-good emotions and some...not so much. I would like to mention a few personal opinions here since this entry is somewhat different than the others in this section. It is about my personal experience of a variety of peoples' perspectives on a single topic.

1- There are probably as many reasons why people "do" Valentine's Day as there are people.
2- Valentine's Day sentiments are not limited to romantic relationships.
3- There may be a couple reasons that seem "out of the spirit of it all," such as pure obligation or fear of reprisal if you opt out.

With that said, my wish is that all who choose to partake in Valentine's Day do so from a place of love. May your participation be an extra acknowledgement, celebrating the feelings and behaviors that have been expressed throughout the year to those you truly care about and appreciate being in your life! Any day, time, or place is available to express genuine love and gratitude to important people in your life, perhaps even a stranger or two. Give kudos to the mail carrier, the person selling newspapers along the side of the road, the bus driver, the restaurant server, the window washer, and the list goes on! I sincerely believe that such gestures will make *you feel great!*

HAPPY VALENTINE'S DAY and may it be filled with love!

Reflections

Since the overarching theme of this book is about feeling good and its benefits, I decided to begin Section 2 with this particular set of happy-news stories. Some stories exemplify the choice to view a potentially unpleasant situation with a pair of "new eyes." I've seen repeatedly that when the slightest reason to feel grateful is noticed and expressed, in any situation, a door opens to allow more opportunities to feel good. In other stories, a person didn't actually shift their perspective, they simply realized they wanted to feel good, so they chose a more positive response to their situation. Additional stories are about a few folks that just seemed to be the kind that had a natural affinity for seeing the "gem" in an otherwise unpleasant situation. Perspective...the real key to feeling great every day...is what they all had in common.

As I looked back on those stories depicting a slight shift in one's viewpoint making such a difference, the concept of kaleidoscopes came to mind. As with a kaleidoscope, a simple twist changes what you see entirely. Just like a simple choice to focus on a happier thought, your whole outlook and level of happiness can change entirely. That's the goal. The bottom line is to be or do whatever it takes to feel good.

"When we are no longer able to change a situation, we are challenged to change ourselves."

— VIKTOR FRANKEL

Chapter 2 – Simple Pleasures

Lemonade Stand Entrepreneur

My daughter Rachel, her wife Megan, and I were driving back from a day of shopping when we passed a little girl managing a lemonade stand. Rachel commented, "Aw, isn't she adorable!?" Megan and I looked at each other and told Rachel to turn around. We double-parked along the street and headed over to check things out. The little salesgirl was a delightful vision with light brown shoulder-length wispy hair and bright green eyes. She was a little on the chubby side with cheeks as rosy as a ripe peach.

"Hi, I'm Natalie and I'm six and I have yummy juice for twenty-five cents. Want some?"

We each replied with a resounding "YES, WE DO!" I handed Natalie $3.00 and told her she could keep the change for being such a great yummy juice seller.

She lit up like a firefly. She shared one more thing about her business. "I'm having such a fun day. Hardly anybody stopped so far. But the sunshine is big and warm and my juice is cold in my pretend refrigerator. Do you guys like it?" She pointed to the large cooler to her left. We all concurred. Rachel and Megan continued to chat and accept a second pouring. I glanced over toward the front door of her house and noticed her mom sitting just inside, overseeing Natalie's venture. She was positioned perfectly to allow her young entrepreneur to maintain a sense of autonomy and still remain safe. Go, Mom!

We finally waved and went back to our car and drove off. I mentioned to the girls how fortunate we were to spot Natalie's stand. You've heard the expression "more bang for your buck." Spending a few minutes with Natalie was worth a fortune. She was enjoying her experience as a "yummy juice seller" to the hilt, paying no mind to the lack of customers. Natalie was a good example of recognizing a simple pleasure for sure.

One Out, One in, and One All Around

One Out, One In

While visiting Union Pacific's Bailey Yard, the world's largest train yard, in North Platte, Nebraska, I had the pleasure of spending a few brief moments with Jessica, the greeter. She shared a delightful incident that had recently occurred at her house. She had two sons who experienced a remarkable event on the same day. Dylan, age seven, LOST his first tooth and Brendyn, almost one, GOT his first tooth! If that wasn't cool enough, it was the same tooth! Jessica took the "tooth-twins" out for ice cream that night. She was so tickled by her good news that her eyes were twinkling. Such a simple yet highly memorable set of events was certainly worth celebrating and sharing! It was easy for me to feel her pride and amazement. Such a fun little anecdote.

One All Around

A particularly enjoyable encounter was with Mr. Tom, a big burly guy and his three-foot puppet pal, Fred. From Fred's crazy tie-dyed outfit and heavy display of jewelry, I gathered he must have been created in the sixties. I had the good fortune to chat with Mr. Tom at the Maryland Line Tractor Show.

He and his cohort had been together twenty plus years participating in local parades, delighting children and adults alike with the antics of Fred. Tom actually restores tractors for a living. He services three main areas in lower Pennsylvania. Having worked for several decades and loving his work, he admitted, "I love my job, always have, but my partnership with Fred is truly what keeps me going. We have a darn good relationship. I 'tell' him what to do and say and he does it with no resistance." Mr. Tom laughed out loud. "No, honestly, the joy we bring to the folks all around, parade or not, makes every breath I take worthwhile. Fred is just the best, ask anyone." Mr. Tom and Fred honored us with a spontaneous performance right there on the spot. It was an unforgettable experience for us as well as the nearby onlookers. I couldn't decide who was funnier, Mr. Tom or Fred! Imagine a man and his puppet lighting up the world around him and beyond. How enchanting it was to chat with a man who spreads joy so lovingly.

Pure Childlike Pride

My new bike tires were dirty! Paradise Campground in Garden Prairie, Illinois, was stellar when it came to walking and biking paths. There was plenty of shade provided by a canopy of trees. That made for perfect conditions to both chill out by the water reading my favorite book and biking without fear of sunstroke. Photo-ops were plentiful and swinging at the playground was a real treat. My first bicycle excursion wasn't just for fun, however. My left handle-bar willingly carried a neatly folded pile of clean laundry in a plastic bag. With my laundry done, I stopped in the restaurant on the grounds and ordered a salad.

Across the room was a young boy of early elementary age sitting with a tall stack of board games in front of him. An older woman who appeared to be his grandmother came by and sat next to him. I overheard a conversation that sounded like happy news. I walked over and introduced myself and asked if I could join them. The woman graciously welcomed me. I told her I was staying there at the campground in the smallest rig of the entire lot of them. She asked if mine was the van with the inspiring quotes all over it. I proudly admitted that it was mine.

"I love that van. I have read each quote first thing in the morning on my way to the showers for the past few days. Did you do that?"

"Yes, mostly. My daughter helped apply several of them."

"Those words are pretty cool, I think. I can even read some of them," the boy chimed in. His grandmother chuckled. I thanked them both.

I asked the young boy his name and what he was up to with all those games. He told me his name was Andrew. He was almost seven years old and he was tall for his age. He also shared that he was on vacation with his grandma and it was a long vacation because they were going to be there all summer. That was the happy news I had overheard earlier.

He shared with me that he comes into the restaurant every day to eat breakfast. Then he goes to the game corner to play, but he can never find what he wants because everything is a big mess. I giggled under my breath. He was so matter-of-fact and quite bewildered for a boy so young.

Andrew explained that he thought about how to fix the problem for a long time and then he "got a lightbulb in his brain." He asked his grandma if she could find any big boxes that he could pile the games in. Not being her first time there, Grandma had developed the right contacts to talk to about filling Andrew's request. She brought him two large Rubbermaid tubs with lids that same morning. He was thrilled with his acquisition. Now he could begin his project.

I asked him what he was going to use the large tubs for. He pointed to a huge container of crayons, a stack of white paper, and a roll of tape.

"I'm going to write the names of the games that I stick in this box and the games I stick in this box on the papers and tape the papers to the right box. So, when I come in here, I can find the game I want to play with. Do you think it's a good idea, Ms. Judi?"

I told him it was a brilliant idea and then asked if he knew what that meant. He said it meant he was really, super smart! We gave each other a thumb's up! He asked me if I wanted to see something pretty cool and before I could respond, he was off running to the closet. When he returned, skidding on the linoleum floor with his new sneakers, he held up a softball about two inches from my face. Andrew blurted out that he got the game ball after his little league game last week before they came to the campground. He showed me with replay motions how he pitched and got two kids out in a row. One was a strike out. The other time, he caught a fly ball.

"I'm a pretty good baseball player, ain't I?" His eyes nearly popped out of their sockets. He came close to me again in a fury and plopped the ball in my lap. "That's the game ball, and the coach gave it to ME!"

51

I clapped loudly and told him he must have been the best player during that game!

He was so pleased with his accomplishment that I could feel his enthusiasm and pride, even as an outsider that wasn't at the game. I could almost see those two precious moments of glory that he was so thrilled about.

We "high-fived" and I told him how happy I was that he told me such great things about himself. I told him he was a great problem solver, an even greater ball player, and how proud I was to have met him. Without hesitation, he asked, "Hey, can I come over and see inside your van?" Gotta love how this young man so effortlessly shifted his focus. What a great example for us adults! I couldn't help but chuckle before I replied. We set up a time for the next day because Grandma was calling him to help in the kitchen. Andrew will likely go far with his "be part of the solution" mindset.

Passion for Art Outside the Box

You have to love Walmart or at least appreciate the diversity of items and customers. I was at one location trying to find decorative duct tape and multicolored pipe cleaners for a project. In the same aisle was a young man who must have noticed my scrunched-up brow and asked what I was looking for so that maybe he could help. What a lovely offer. His genius recommendation was for me to check for the duct tape on the other end of the store in either hardware or near kitchen. I laughed out loud. "Now why would I think it would be in with arts and crafts? Thanks!" I did find the pipe cleaners in the arts and crafts department though!

I noticed the man had a basket filled with a smorgasbord of artsy supplies. I couldn't resist inquiring what kind of project he might be working on. "I'm a freelance artist. Much of my work has been commissioned by friends and family and others by word of mouth. Many other projects I create simply because of the pure joy of it." He shared that he especially loves creating masterpieces using a variety of mediums. He put the hand basket down and went on to say, "Using a multimedia approach seems to bring the piece to life. There's the magic of expression from your imagination, creative talent, emotions, and personal vision. Helping otherwise nonrelated items come together like they were destined to comingle is what gets me going. And the beauty of art is that there's no right or wrong. Wow, am I rambling?"

I assured him he was not. I was blown away by his passion and spontaneous sharing. His face was alive with twinkling eyes, a flushed tone to his skin, and hand gestures that resembled the fluidity of art itself. We chatted a few minutes longer about the importance of dabbling in some type of creative, outside the box, endeavor with reckless abandon just for the fun of it.

I told him he reminded me of an excited kindergartener with hands saturated in finger paints kneeling in front of a giant piece of white paper. We laughed out loud. I thanked him for hanging out with me and adding a spark to my creative juices. We parted ways, both feeling more alive. I headed to the hardware department in search of the duct tape which seemed like a quest for the Holy Grail.

Nature and All Its Glory

There are precious few times that are more magnificent than feeling one with nature. The connectedness, for me, wakes up my soul to remembering that everything is made from the same energy – the stars, the ocean, the earth, the snow and you and me. That knowing gives me a sense of peace and excitement simultaneously. I'm able to envision all of life shrinking down small enough to be contained within my body. Other times, I can feel myself expand to reach the outer limits of the universe.

I have included below a description of three scenes. After you read each one, take a minute to close your eyes and try to be there and feel the magic of the simple pleasure of being with nature.

A - Autumn along Skyline Drive in Virginia is when the beauty of the season is at its peak. The leaves are gorgeous even on an overcast day. Glancing out over the mountain tops, what I saw was what appeared to be an explosion of Skittles across the sky. Rich shades of gold, crimson, green, saffron, and chocolate sprinkled the tree line set up against a rich clear blue cloudless sky. Nothing was moving. It was as if it had been painted and placed before me to admire. It nearly took my breath away.

B - I continued to drive to Dark Hollow Falls where I hiked a half mile straight down to reach a waterfall. It was spectacular, well worth the trek. Layers upon layers of water crashing over rocks, flying in many directions, and crossing each other on the way down the seventy-foot drop. The water seemed to be kissed by the bright sun creating sparkling diamond chips from the droplets bouncing across one another into the air. Quite a crowd was gathered around the railed platform at the base of the cascade taking pictures. I found a spot off to the side where I could watch the excited faces of children who surely dreamed of jumping in to splash and play. The adults were as mesmerized as the little ones. I was close enough to overhear a few comments from people who were seeing their first waterfall. The oohs and aahs were delightful. With all the commotion going on around me, I was amazed at how still I was able to feel inside. Something magical happens around naturally flowing water, be it the ocean, a waterfall, or a lively river. The sounds resonate with me on a deep spiritual level. It's a life-affirming event that allows me to tune out any extraneous noises and become one with the flow. I remained absorbed in the experience for quite a while until I knew I had received what I didn't know I came for, and it felt great.

C - I made a one-night stop at Thousand Trails Campground in Lebanon, Pennsylvania. It was dark when I arrived and the morning brought a gloriously foggy lake. I got comfy in one of the lounge chairs and watched my surroundings change over the course of an hour. At first, the only thing visible was a nearby bush at the edge of the shoreline about ten feet away. Gradually, the once thick white blanketed sky and lake gave way to a paradise of autumn-kissed trees caressing a few homes on a small island across the lake. That gradual revelation felt akin to a blank sheet of paper becoming a beautiful sentiment or a canvas destined to evolve into a masterpiece at the hand of the artist. Once my eyes were content with that sweet expression of nature's magic, I leaned back in my chair and lowered my eyelids to allow myself to absorb it all. During my time of stillness, I did some deep breathing which always enhances my experience. I was about to open my eyes when, the magnificent sound of a bald eagle's call graced my ears beckoning me to glance upward immediately. There, soaring along the tree line, I witnessed a mature eagle in all its white-feathered glory. What a spectacular sight! My gaze was fixed on its graceful movements as it danced with the breeze before perching on a tall tree. From where I was, its head and tail looked like cotton balls mounted on the newly visible azure sky. "Oh, what a beautiful morning. Oh, what a beautiful day..."

Reflections

Often life gets a little crazy, and you feel like you are running on an adult hamster wheel, but you must not allow anything that feels good, no matter how small, to go by as insignificant. The word pleasure rhymes with treasure. Sometimes, a simple pleasure must be sought out in the midst of a seemingly ordinary day just as treasures are searched for by those seeking gold. Any acknowledgment of a good feeling is your gold.

Here are a few examples of simple pleasures during my travels that could have gone unnoticed or considered no big deal. I chose to give them their moment of glory for providing me occasions to feel great and be grateful.

1- Little messages from songs on the radio were gifted to me throughout my first month on the road, invoking an "Oh yeah!"
2- Random thoughts appeared that kept me strong in my knowledge that I made the best choice for me.
3- Strangers jumping at the chance to share their good news, and their overall response to me, gave me the feeling that my mission was a worthwhile and timeless endeavor.
4- Van-Go was my means of making my dream come true and spread joy as she rolled. Drivers beeped and gave me a thumbs-up when they read the quotes on the sides of my van. People even stopped or asked me to stop so they could take pictures.
5- Other signs that I was on the right path included the fact that "trouble" only happened when I was someplace safe and knew the area well enough to make a connection and I was never caught in the rain during a problem.

There were many more instances that filled my heart with gratitude. Recognizing these tidbits helped confirm my beliefs that everything always works out well for me and that I am always safe.

"Sometimes the smallest things take up the most room in your heart."

— WINNIE-THE-POOH

Chapter 3 - Courage

A Brave Disclosure

It was dusk and the sky was a pale gray. I was sitting in my van at the campground area in Niobrara State Park in Nebraska in mid-September! Not a living soul or RV was there. My heart skipped a beat. This place was vast and I felt sort of lost in a vacuum.

My reservation was for twelve days. I wondered if it would become more alive during my stay. I took in a deep breath, closed my eyes, and tried to see in my mind's eye a more soothing scenario. I was being surrounded by children roasting marshmallows over a campfire, families riding bikes, and someone in the distance, lying in a hammock reading a good book. I longed for the sights and sounds of community, especially laughter. I wasn't accustomed to this much solitude. It was getting dark and all I wanted to do was sleep.

The sun was peeking over the tree line as I was waking up. A golden glow permeated the windows of my little home. I opened the door to check the weather. A man in a uniform came around the bend driving a Jeep. I was thrilled to see another human and I waved him down. He stopped and introduced himself as Joe from the Knox County Police Department. He was making his twice-daily rounds through the park. He satisfied my question about the emptiness. Turkey hunting season had just ended and that was why it was so desolate.

Joe was intrigued by the quotes on Van-Go. He wanted to know about them and offered to give me a private tour of the grounds so I could tell him as we were driving. I laughed because I was planning to ask him if he had anything good going on in his life to share. Truth be told, my ulterior motive was to keep him around awhile for company sake! I jumped in his vehicle and off we went exploring. I told him about my adventure and how the van got to be decorated.

At first, it was to cover the whiteness. Then it evolved into a desire to provide "inspiration-on-the-go." I wanted other drivers and folks sitting on their porches or waiting for a bus to read a quote or two and smile as Van-Go and I went by. He loved my story and thanked me for sharing.

"Okay, it's your turn. Tell me something cool in your life." His head perked up and a huge smile appeared. His story began with him having had several unsuccessful relationships over the years. The last one involved a childless marriage by mutual choice. He had a vasectomy to ensure their chosen lifestyle wouldn't be derailed by an unwanted pregnancy. For a moment or two, his expression flattened and his story paused. Then once again the smile was refreshed and his lustrous eyes widened. "But now for the good part!" My heart was beginning to beat a little bit faster with anticipation. What came next brought tears to my eyes.

He had gotten divorced from his first wife and a year later met the woman he knew he was destined to be with forever. He described her as simply beautiful in every way. As their relationship blossomed and more about their dreams and goals came to light, the discussion ensued about how many children she had always imagined having. Joe said he never felt so much pain in his heart in his life. How was he going to tell her he couldn't give her that lifelong dream? He couldn't bear the thought of losing her. He had proposed only a few months earlier. Joe knew he had to tell his beautiful fiancé the whole story despite the possible consequences.

He managed to muster up enough fortitude to divulge the potential deal-breaker news. His fiancé was much calmer than he anticipated. They discussed him having a reverse vasectomy performed and to keep positive thoughts. She let him know beforehand that if it didn't work, they could always adopt children. That eased his trembling heart. Joe stopped the vehicle, looked directly into my already tear-stained eyes, and exclaimed, "Only nineteen days after the surgery, the love of my life and I conceived our first child and we're due in three and a half short months just in time for Christmas!" We hugged out of gratitude and excitement for the miracle they experienced. By then we both had tears of joy trickling down our faces. I waved to Joe twice a day when he made his rounds. I felt a connection with him somehow and it felt good.

The remaining ten days of my non-refundable stay at the park were spent enjoying nature with a new perspective about solitude. I reveled in the simplicity of my own company. My surroundings didn't feel as empty anymore *and* there was new life on the horizon.

Enjoy *your* own company. After all, you are unmistakably amazing!

Triumph of Determination

Craving my morning caffeine fix, I passed a full-sized restaurant and got in the Starbuck's drive-through with half the county! While patiently waiting for my turn at the order window, I noticed a sign in my rearview mirror that read FIRST WATCH. That was the restaurant I had passed, so I wiggled out of line, parked, and went inside. The usual set up of tables and chairs was full. The bar that accommodated ten had one spot open. I scurried over and hopped up on the last seat! My face was quickly buried in the menu. When I finally put the menu down, there was a smiling face in its place. We both said, "Good morning." Before long, we had begun an interesting conversation.

"Hi, I'm Trey, born and raised in Florida. I'm twenty-one, and I'm in a particularly grand mood this morning. How about you?"

"My name is Judi, and I'm sixty-two and traveling around the country in a van seeking out good news from people I meet."

"Well, Ms. Judi, you sat in the right seat."

"Okay, then, wutcha got for me?"

We both laughed.

"I just purchased my very first boat! I'm a third-generation fishing guide. I guess I've always known that was what I wanted to be. It's probably in the blood." He chuckled.

I expressed my interest and enthusiasm and asked how it worked. He explained joyfully in great detail. Then his demeanor shifted considerably. He began to fiddle with his coffee stir and lost eye contact for a moment or two. I waited. He went on to tell me that he had been in the Army for a year, stationed at Fort Hood.

"Um, some pretty horrific things happened while I was in, and I kind of shut down. I was diagnosed with depression, and they wanted me to take drugs. When I refused, they discharged me. I was determined to work it out without the damn pharmaceuticals. In my family, there's a history of, well, anyway I just did. I saw a therapist and she taught me about meditation. Between the sessions and my new spiritual practice, I'm doing great now. I'm so glad I decided not to take the drugs. I knew I could do it without them. My own fishing boat - WOW! Since my job allows for a flexible schedule, when I'm not on the boat, I really love to race with my Harley and hunt."

I told Trey how happy I was for him and his new fishing boat and how courageous I thought he was for being true to himself by finding his own way of healing. He thanked me and said he was also happy that I got the very last seat! We laughed loud enough to turn a few heads. I asked if he wanted to see my home on wheels. We went out to the parking lot and I gave him the three-minute tour! He loved it. We shook hands and went our separate ways, both feeling pleased with our brief but special conversation.

Women on a Mission

Leaving from an afternoon at the beach, I swung by my friend Sharon's for a quick visit before I got on the road again. She had company and there were introductions around the table. It was funny that I wasn't even thinking about finding a feel-good story but, sure enough, I stumbled into two of them!

The two friends of Sharon's were Reg and Janet. They were in the middle of a discussion that I seem to have fallen into without creating much disturbance. Sharon introduced me and I said hello and sat down quietly. She snuck a glass of wine in front of me. Reg was holding the "talking stick" and was giving kudos to her kids. Her daughter, Julie was in her first year of law school at Emory in Atlanta, Georgia and her son, Matt just started his third year at Virginia Tech.

"Not to brag...oh what the hell, I am proud of them. They're both smart, funny, and live with integrity. What more could a parent ask for?" Reg was the kind of parent who stressed to her kids the importance of being able to take care of yourself financially. She was on a mission to do whatever it took to become debt-free to set an example for her children. The determination in her voice was palpable. Sharon and I both commended her on her philosophy and her gutsy plan and wished her the best.

I noticed that Janet hadn't chimed in much. As it turned out, Janet was in a state of flux. She explained how she was vacillating between feeling proud of herself and still grieving for her husband of forty-five years who passed away over eight years ago. I asked what made her feel proud.

Sharon walked over and gave Janet a huge hug and said, "Go ahead, girl, tell her."

Janet raised her head a little and hesitated a moment before she began to speak. "Well, this is the first time since I've been widowed that I made a choice to do anything by myself. I was always afraid I would feel alone, but I planned a vacation by myself for myself." All of us cheered with loud voices and a sip of wine!

"I have been here at Sharon's for three weeks, and I can't seem to make myself leave. I'm having too much fun to go home." Laughter filled the room!

My heart swelled with compassion and appreciation for her newfound courage, for stepping out of her comfort zone and making a choice to take care of herself. I only imagined what it must be like to learn to live a completely different kind of life than you had for forty-five years. Reaching a point in your grieving process when you can feel something better and are able to live your own life again is a moment to treasure.

A Life of Courage

Since I retired, I've especially loved opportunities to engage with and learn about the ways that nature not only takes care of itself, but also takes care of us. I took a tour at the Kanapaha Botanical Gardens in Gainesville, Florida. The experience left me with an even greater sense of awe of nature's perfection.

After the tour, I headed to my next overnight spot, The Dixieland Music & RV Park in Waldo, Florida. Greg and Joy greeted me as I arrived just before dinner time. I noticed that Joy had a patch over her right eye, but it didn't impede her taking care of my registration packet or her pleasant disposition. Greg made sure I parked in just the right space and got set up okay. Their hospitality continued with a recommendation for dinner at a local diner and a stroll through the huge indoor flea market across the street. Dinner was wonderful and I had a blast at the flea market. I didn't get anything because of my new minimalist lifestyle.

The next morning, I went by the office to say thanks and good-bye. Joy smiled and began to offer an unsolicited account of her pre-camp-host life. As I listened to the ways Joy had enthusiastically participated in her life, I was moved. For thirty years, she was a catastrophic event manager where her duties included coordinating teams of doctors, attorneys, insurance companies, and case managers to ensure that the proper treatment and care was given to anyone who had been involved in a life-altering accident. Joy told me about her most cherished success story. A young man in his twenties lost his arm in a machinery accident. She orchestrated the acquisition of his prothesis after a period of healing and made modifications to his home as well. Best of all, she contacted his "old boss" and arranged for the young man to be rehired as a safety manager.

She went back to school for her GED at age thirty-nine and continued to college where she earned a couple of degrees. In 1967, she even ran an orphanage for fifty girls and started a church in Port au Prince, Haiti. At that point, I was already impressed with her strength of character alone. I admired her brave spirit even more when she told me her right eye had been removed two weeks ago because of a serious cataract condition. She was waiting for it to heal enough to be fitted for a new prosthetic eye.

"It's been a little challenging, but I'm so grateful to at least have perfect vision in my left eye." *That is one woman who knows how to find a good-feeling thought to be grateful for.*

Everything she shared was with the most beautiful smile. She thanked me for letting her talk. I was at a loss for words, so I just hugged her.

The Triumphant Human Spirit

I had the pleasure of talking to a man one evening who had much to share. Hani was born in Jerusalem. His family dwelling had no electricity and no water. At the age of four, his parents moved to Kuwait but Hani stayed behind with his grandparents at his request.

Over the three years he lived there, several unfortunate events took place. First, he broke his arm. A man who took care of everyone's animals (with no formal education) set it with a piece of old wood and rags. It actually healed. Next, he fell and cut open the top of his head at age five. There was so much blood that his grandmother thought for sure he would bleed to death. There were no doctors, no anesthetics, and no stitches. She applied fresh coffee grounds as a salve, wrapped his head with fabric, propped him up, and prayed for two weeks. It healed but left an oddly-shaped scar. Then, at age seven, he and his friends "stole" figs, olives, and tomatoes from his grandfather's garden and sold them to people. They got caught and that was the last straw for his grandparents. They shipped him off to Kuwait to be with his parents.

When he arrived, everything around him was foreign and he kind of freaked out. He sat and stared at the lights. He put his sandals in the fridge, thinking it was a closet. He kept wanting to feel the running water. He tried to get inside the back of the television to be with the tiny people in there! At some point, his parents sat him down and explained about everything that was so foreign to Hani.

After high school, he wanted desperately to go to America. His mother forbade it because she knew that if he did, he would never come home. They did agree for him to go to school in England. That only lasted six months because the gloomy climate caused Hani to become depressed. He secretly applied for a VISA and was turned down twice. Finally, on his third attempt, it was granted and he came to America without his parents' blessing. That was forty years ago. He went to college and obtained a couple of degrees, made quite a bit of money but lost it all when his cousin and business partner embezzled from

66

their company. He built his life and business back up, but then the big stock market crash destroyed him. Finally, a third effort held up, and he was doing well and was financially secure.

Hani's was an interesting story, perhaps, even inspiring. Well, the next phase of our conversation went in an entirely different direction. It was that piece that caused a grown man to cry like a baby in the company of a perfect stranger. His sharing caused him to relive much of the pain and struggle he endured for a seven-year period. During that conversation, I felt a deeper connection to humanity and its myriad of complexities. The oneness among people that we so often forget about showed itself to me clearly and profoundly. It was difficult to keep my composure while feeling such compassion for a fellow human being. My heart was aching for him. I've left out most of the horrific details, but enough of his experience is here for you to get the gist of it.

At age thirty-three, Hani got a woman pregnant. He was Muslim, and she was Catholic, leaving him with the belief that the only solution was to wed. He promised her that he would take care of everything. Throughout the pregnancy all went very smoothly. He bought a house, and they were looking forward to what seemed like a situation that just might work out after all. She delivered their daughter via C-section but three days later, she "snapped." Her behavior and moods were extremely erratic. She even became violent toward Hani. Both of her sisters were doctors and they told him to be patient with her, as some women go through a rough emotional period after giving birth. They also recommended psychiatric counseling. So, Hani did the best he could and paid for the best doctors for his wife.

As difficult as the next several years were, they remained married because he had also promised his wife her green card. She was from Mexico. It took four years! Once she had what she needed, the marriage dissolved. She wanted her freedom. He did his best to convince her to stay but to no avail. After she left, he never remarried. He spent the next seven grueling years in and out of courtrooms trying to get shared custody of their daughter. This all happened

67

shortly after 9/11. Being Muslim made the entire process rather complicated, since the mother of his child, who also did his company's books, began making horrendous false accusations. The two at the top of her list were tax evasion and child abuse. He was devastated. This man was investigated thoroughly by Homeland Security, Child Protective Services, as well as several other agencies for seven long years! Had it not been for a large community of citizens who testified on his behalf, Hani would likely have been put in prison. Fortunately, the accusations were deemed unsubstantiated. When he spoke of how he nearly lost the only truly blessed thing in his life, his daughter, and what he went through to be able to even see her, he wept.

After many years of getting to know each other, Nadia, age twenty-six, was extremely close to her dad. He considers himself the luckiest man in the world. When his daughter graduated from St. Mary's University in San Antonio, he paid for her to go to Jerusalem to spend time with her paternal grandmother who was eighty-two. That meant a great deal to all three of them. Nadia had recently married when we talked. Hani gladly told me she cherishes her new husband *and* her brave and loving dad. She tells him often how much of an inspiration he has been to her.

I believe that any account of what the human spirit endures for the sake of love, integrity, and appreciation is nothing short of miraculous. Hani's story touched me deeply and I will forever be grateful to him for the effect he had on my heart. By the way, the day he shared his story was the day after Hani's fifty-ninth birthday! I wished him not only a happy birthday, but many more days filled with the love and joy he so rightly deserved.

Reflections

Just entertaining the idea of doing something you aren't sure will work out or attempting an action that's outside your comfort zone could possibly cause you to feel anxious or doubtful. Perhaps such a notion would excite you, encourage you, energize you, and make you feel great. Either way, going for it and achieving success at something is cause to be proud! If you were passionate enough to embark on an undertaking whose outcome couldn't be foreseen and risked it, even though it scared you a bit, you had a goal worthy of your time and effort. Be sure to recognize your accomplishment and celebrate it. You'll love the way you feel.

The people in the above stories demonstrated courage in a variety of ways. No one was any greater or lesser than the other. All of them powerfully impacted their lives in ways that changed them for the better. In some cases, one person's courage extended beyond themselves to enrich the lives of those around them. Being courageous doesn't mean you have to overcome a monumental obstacle like Rosa Parks, Martin Luther King, or Joan of Arc did. Simple acts of courage might include trying a new food, speaking to a stranger, standing up for a person being bullied, getting a new hairstyle, or simply getting up an hour earlier than usual to exercise or meditate. It's really about showing up for your life full speed ahead with your eyes wide open and your heart all-in!

> *"Bran thought about it. 'Can a man still be brave if he's*
> *afraid?' 'That is the only time a man can be brave,'*
> *his father told him."*
> — GEORGE R. R. MARTIN, GAME OF THRONES

Chapter 4 – Family

Glowing Waitress

After an early walk on a beach one Sunday morning, I stopped for breakfast at a Friendly's Restaurant and was fortunate enough to have Maria as my server. What a pleasant and unpretentious woman! She was a delight from the moment she said hello. I placed my order and, like on several other occasions, I got the impression she might have a bit of happy news to share. I'm good at reading people and she had happy written all over her! After I ate my delicious breakfast of eggs over medium and a short stack with fresh fruit, I had a quick moment to mention my Bright Spots. She said she'd love to tell me something and she would be right back. She arranged to take her break early and sat across from me in the booth. Right off the bat, she exclaimed, "I love my job...well, it's not really a job, job; it's more like an amazing opportunity to chat with people on vacation. Everyone on vacation is happy!"

Maria went on to ask if she could share more than one cool thing about her life. I smiled and nodded. She had been married a little over twenty years and was so proud of her family, which consisted of a great husband and two super kids. Her son Terry was seventeen and her daughter Lauren was eight. Her hubby, whose age she chose not to disclose, was Brian. They had been through some pretty rough times, but the wonderful thing about them was that they always managed to stick together no matter what type of challenge they were faced with. "Now how many families can say that?" she asked, beaming with pride.

"Not as many as we would all like, I suppose."

Maria continued telling me what a gem her husband was. He took care of everything on the home front at night when she was at school three times a week. "I've been studying to become a nurse with a smile that will work as well as any medicine to make my patients feel better, lighter, and more alive."

She was glowing as she shared her dream. Maria glanced up and her boss was waving her back to the kitchen. "Oh, I have to go. It sure was nice meeting you."

She jumped up and was gone in a flash. I didn't have a chance to let her know how nice it was for ME to have been on the receiving end of her love and appreciation for family, life, and herself. I wrote "Thank you" on the check and left a little extra with the tip. I walked to my car feeling lighter than when I went into the restaurant thanks to Maria.

The Joys of Having Pre-school Children

The pleasure of engaging in a conversation with Kathi, who served up the most amazing burger I've had in fifty-six years, would turn out to be the highlight of my day. She was absolutely effervescent in her appearance and character. Her uniform collar and upper bodice were decked out with award pins and happy thought buttons. Her voice was cheerful and welcoming, and her smile alone practically spoke to you, saying, "Hi, I'm Kathi, a very happy woman and I can't wait to serve you and make you happy too."

When she delivered my mega burger, I asked her to please stop back and sit with me a minute when she had some down time because I had a question for her. She said she would be back in about five minutes because that was the start of her break. When she returned, I had finished half of my scrumptious burger and was full. She offered to wrap the other half to take with me. She was back in a flash with my "doggie bag" and sat down. I complimented her on her cheerful disposition and how it made me feel welcomed. She smiled. Then I told her about my mission to have people share good news in their lives as I traveled and that I had an inkling she might have something to share. If so, I'd be thrilled to hear about it.

Wiggling a little in her seat, she quickly responded with the fact that yesterday was her thirtieth birthday and how excited she was to be rolling into a new decade of her life. She paused, then reached into her apron pocket and pulled out a piece of folded white paper, opened it and began to read what was on the inside. "Mommy, I love your curly hair and cute smile." Kathi told me that precious message was from her five-year-old son, Landon. With the assistance of his grandma, he created his very first birthday card for his mommy. A small tear still tucked inside her lower lid glistened as she said, "He just melts my heart all the time."

I acknowledged her joy with a smile and a gentle touch to her hand. I asked if she had any other children. "I sure do," she exclaimed. "My little pipsqueak Ava is three and she's totally enamored with the movie *Frozen.* Her favorite character is Princess Elsa and as young as Ava is, she seems to have memorized nearly every word Elsa spoke. I love it when she gets in the Princess stance and breaks out in song, 'Do you want to build a snowman?' This display of pure toddlerness often occurs in public when I least expect it. I haven't heard any complaints yet, so that's good!" We both laughed.

I asked if she was always this exuberant and she honestly said she was not. "Not every day is perfect, you know? But when I feel like the day is headed into a downward spiral, I stop and think of my kids and the weirdest thing often happens. My day turns around and I can usually find at least one thing to be happy about in my day that seemed lost."

Thoughts of appreciation for family, especially children, can have a miraculous effect on your day when you choose to recognize it at a moment when you need to feel better. Pretty awesome! Pretty easy!

Mom Saves the Day

While getting my nails done the day before my son's wedding, I had the good fortune to have Regine as my manicurist. As often happens, a conversation between us ensued. She told me how her six-year-old daughter Evolet had been asking for a goldfish for months. Finally, good old Mom took her to pick out two bright orange fish along with a bowl, a plastic plant, colorful stones, and a small can of fish food.

"Oh, my goodness! You would have thought it was Christmas morning. Evolet couldn't be still enough to help assemble the tank. She just cradled the plastic bag of goldfish in her arms like they were newborn babies! As soon as I plopped the little swimmers into the tank, Evolet began a bonding ritual. She whispered to them, offering them names to see if they liked them, and sharing her innermost secrets. She fed them two times each day, watching and waiting for the flakes to disappear into Gus and Gabby's teeny mouths. Every time I observed this sweet interaction, my heart overflowed with love."

Regine fed them before school and said "Good morning" to Gus and Gabby because she and Evolet were always in a rush. Fortunately, Evolet was okay with allowing Mom to do that. By this time, I was in stitches chuckling with delight. Regine had to remind me to keep my hands still so as not to smear the polish!

Then the tone of the conversation shifted when Regine explained that she noticed very early one morning about two weeks ago, that Gus and Gabby were no longer "with us." She rushed to get Evolet out the door to catch the bus. Then Regine scrambled to secure the lifeless pair inside a Ziploc baggie. She drove to the pet store and begged the assistant to find a new set that matched the original pair. She knew Evolet would be devastated if she knew her little buddies had perished. Regine was in no way ready to handle that one!

The loving deception was successful. Evolet sprinted to the fish tank after school to greet and feed and chat with Gus and Gabby, smiling as brightly as she had the night before the unmentionable occurred. Regine was inexplicably relieved and took in a deep breath when she watched Evolet spend time with her friends with such childlike innocence. "Six is just too young; ya know?" Regine uttered.

I simply nodded my head affirmatively. I felt such compassion for Mom as she shared her story. My nails were done, and Regine walked me to the drying station and thanked me for listening. She explained she hadn't told anyone else. I smiled.

Training Wheels Begone!

Mountaindale Cabins and RV Resort in Colorado Springs, Colorado, afforded me more than one wonderful experience. After I returned from a beautiful, early morning stroll through the expansive wilderness surrounding the area, I stopped to relax, leaning up against a tree that must have been three feet in diameter. Moments later, I heard a slight stirring near me. About fifty feet away, looking directly at me, stood a white-speckled doe chomping leaves with her ears perked up toward the pre-dawn sky. She appeared to almost smile at me, so I smiled back, of course. I was overjoyed.

At breakfast, my server Cassy delivered my meal with a smile. The restaurant wasn't busy, so I asked her right out if she had any good news about her life to share.

"Oh, I don't know. I never really gave it much thought. Let me think about it," she replied and walked back toward the kitchen. The next thing I knew, she was standing beside me with a twinkle in her eye and a smile much broader than even before.

It seemed she had thought of something cool to share. The week before, her five-year-old son Ethan learned to ride his two-wheeler without the training wheels. I concurred that it was indeed great news. I told her I knew she must be proud of him.

"Proud as any mom could be. He has been so brave. He got right back up each time he fell over during the first three weeks after we took the training wheels off. Last week, when he rode almost ten feet before he toppled over, he jumped up and yelled, 'Mommy, I did it! I'm a big boy now.'"

She re-enacted the scene depicting Ethan shooting his arms above his head with his fists pumping in the air jumping with both feet off the ground. She was glowing. Cassy created a wave of giggling around the restaurant as customers reacted having no idea what was going on. It was great! Joy spreading like dandelion 'puffballs' in a windstorm is a fabulous thing to witness. I thanked her for sharing such a memorable moment with me. She headed to another table while I continued enjoying my breakfast. I chuckled before my next bite, recalling my own kids' moments of glory at their two-wheel success. I finished eating and took care of my check. I noticed that I chuckled a few more times later in the day reminiscing Cassy's childlike antics.

Bubbly Alice and Crew

My scooter and I spent a day taking in the sites in Marianna, Florida. It made for an all-day excursion and rendered me satisfied, but tired and hungry. I grabbed a shower and rode my scooter into town to Bobbi's Waffle Iron, a local diner recommended by the staff at the park. Breakfast was served twenty-four hours and I love breakfast food any time of day. How did the woman at the office know that place would be the perfect choice? Excited to see the menu, I ordered a homemade waffle with fresh fruit and a ham slice on the side. My mouth was watering just placing my order! Looking out the window, it felt strange having breakfast in the dark.

Bubbly Alice was my server. I gave her that nickname unbeknownst to her because she was absolutely effervescent in her interactions with every customer she waited on. Broad smiles, thank yous, you're welcomes, chats with toddlers, and a pep in her step summoned that nickname.

I finished my scrumptious meal and played Scrabble on my phone until the diner cleared out a little. When Bubbly came over to see if I wanted anything else, I said I would like to talk with her a minute when she got the chance. She was eager to accommodate me without even knowing why and sat down across from me in the booth.

"Perfect timing, ma'am. You're my last customer. My shift is finally over."

After I complimented her on her cheery disposition and efficient service, I told her about my good-news mission. She threw her hands up in the air and said, "You wanna know what lights me up? Right there in the seat by the register: my only grandchild, Michelle. She's fourteen."

I turned enough to see Michelle waiting for her grandmother to get off work. She had a sweet smile on her face. "C'mon over here, darlin'," Alice called to the young girl. Alice scooted over so Michelle could join us at the booth.

I introduced myself to Michelle. Alice put her arm around the girl and shared that she had been homeschooled since day one and that she adored the time with her grandmother. The love emanating from this woman was palpable. It wouldn't have surprised me to find out the entire restaurant was affected by it.

I told Alice she was a glowing light in that diner. Unexpectedly, I heard another voice from around the corner. Jerry, Alice's husband overheard my comment.

As a reminder to her and news for me, he declared that HE was the light around the whole family no matter where any of them were!

"Yep. He means it too, ma'am. And he's righter than the sun rising every morning. He likes to tease me about it whenever he gets the opportunity. He keeps us all smiling no matter what the weather inside or out. His nickname around town is 'Jolly Jerry.'"

We all chuckled over that one. I leaned across the table and whispered to Michelle that I had privately nicknamed her grandmother 'Bubbly Alice.' Michelle and I laughed. Alice just smiled and Jerry coaxed them on so he could get them home, since we had chatted right past Michelle's bedtime.

Grammy and Grandsons Go Camping

Three days to get ready for three days to get crazy! I invited my two grandsons, Cameron and Jay, to hang out with me at the campground where I was staying. Muddy Run Park in Holtwood, Pennsylvania, was only an hour or so from where my daughter Nicole lived. Before their arrival, there was much to do to prepare for their visit. I discovered that seven-year-old boys required much more planning than I had thought when I first threw out the idea. Kid food and lots of it and enough fun activities to keep them happy, yet safe enough to keep Grammy happy! So, I stocked the fridge with bologna, bread, ketchup, squeezable yogurt, peanut butter and jelly and milk! In the pantry were the basic staples for a second grader's diet – Pop Tarts, cheeseballs, honey sticks, Fruity Pebbles, Cocoa Puffs, and all the fixings for s'mores (chocolate bars, marshmallows, and graham crackers). A complimentary visit to the dentist should have come with that grocery order. Oh, my!

The activities list turned out to be much longer than the grocery list. One of the hikes I planned to take them on had become questionable because it rained heavily the night before they were due to arrive, so I hiked the trail myself early that morning. Good foresight, Grammy! It would have been at least a two-hour hike on slushy and varied terrain for three miles, had I not turned around about thirty minutes in. THAT got scratched off the activity list fast.

Plenty of firewood was also on the necessities list. The day before the boys arrived, I hopped on my bike and rode to the office to pick up a bundle of logs. I don't know what I was thinking! There was no way I was going to be able to strap those logs anywhere on my bike and ride the ups and downs back to the van. I was in a quandary. No one was around to lend a hand or a truck! I saw no options but to bungee the logs to my basket and walk the load back to my campsite. Off I went, holding onto the handlebars of a bike that was front-heavy, through what felt like an obstacle course. An hour later, I arrived at the van completely drenched from the strain and the humidity. The latter of which

I had conveniently forgotten about having lived in New Mexico for four years. Nevertheless, I was now ready for the boys, or so I thought.

Nicole pulled into the campsite with what appeared like human jumping beans in the back seat. "Quick, open the door before they hurt themselves," my daughter warned. They unloaded all their gear, kissed Mom goodbye and wanted to know when we were going to eat and what we were going to do for three days. I helped them unwind by taking a walk collecting pine cones. They were great fire starters for our campfires.

We had a blast together all three days playing at the playground, eating frequently, catching lightning bugs, coloring, paddle boating, building campfires, and I could go on and on.

One of the two highlights, according to the boys, was spending time at the lake. We watched gaggles of geese walk in and out of the lake squawking while we laughed at their silliness. Once, we watched fifteen humongous geese glide in toward the shoreline, get out as usual, expecting them to mosey around the shoreline. That time however, they waddled right toward us. We figured they would just go around us, but, NO! We were surrounded and they were "yelling" at us! Truth be told, it was a little frightening. They were such big geese, and they were not happy with us. The boys were emotionally torn between fear and excitement. This was indeed the first time they had been held hostage by a gaggle of geese. After about twenty minutes of deafening noise, I told the boys to stand up slowly and follow me. I used my sunhat to shoo them away, repeating, "Go, go, go." A risky maneuver, I knew, but we had to try something. Fortunately, they slowly spread out and allowed safe passage to the trailhead that led us back to our site. The boys talked about that for months.

The second event can only be referred to as "Bombarding Grammy." Their sleeping area was a loft that sat on the rim across the width of the van and was positioned directly over my sofa bed. They stayed up much later than I did each night watching DVDs on a portable player or playing with their matchbox cars. One night they decided to play Army with a full box of tissues. One at a time, they scrunched up a tissue and dropped it down through the crack between their space and mine. Each one landed either on my head or darn close to it. They thought this was a great game. I slept through the entire bombardment. I woke up surrounded by tissue bombs! I had to laugh. I woke them up and told them it was time for breakfast and to get ready for today's adventure. They jumped up and came sliding down the back of the loft. Pointing to the massive pile of tissue, I told them that their adventure was going to have to happen before breakfast. First, I asked about how those could have possibly gotten where they were, and they explained their game. We all laughed, and I gave them noogies on their heads. Then, I had them pick up each one, smooth it out and place it back in the tissue box. That box became for their use only!

My personal highlight with them was twofold. The first was listening to them laugh so hard they almost cried on multiple occasions. The second was in the evenings when they were worn out from the day's activities and we sat around the fire talking about our day and what their favorite parts were. It was multi-generational magic and I'm grateful for every second of those few days we had together.

Reflections

You can feel good about many aspects of family. They can provide comfort, pride, loyalty, friendship, lessons, encouragement, laughter, and support whether you live together or not. Families come in all shapes and sizes, colors and configurations, and every member has merit. Several types of families were in the stories you read. There were children, grandchildren, parents, and grandparents. Every one of them experienced love regarding their particular family make-up and was eager to share a happy thought.

Look for and appreciate the opportunities to feel good about whatever kind of family you have and let your smile spill over onto someone you care about. I bet if you pay close enough attention, you'll see something you hadn't seen before in each member of your family. Let them know!

Try this fun activity to amp up your appreciation of a family member: You don't even need to be in the presence of your chosen person. First, think about your person in great detail. You can begin with physical appearance, then move on to memories you have about things they've done or said that made you smile. If they're someone you already like, this game will feel easier. If you're on the outs with them, it may take a little longer. What the heck, do it anyway. The next step is to observe the same person when you're with them. See if you notice anything you missed during the first part of the game and if how you feel about them changed at all.

Potential benefits: You will see that person in a new light. Your appreciation for them will increase. You will feel good when you think of them. Respect for them and their overall likeability may improve.

> *"The family, that dear octopus from whose tentacles we never quite escape, nor, in our inmost hearts, ever quite wish to."*
>
> — DODI SMITH

Chapter 5 – The Accident

An April Fools' Prank – Not Hardly

Once upon a time, on April first, an otherwise intelligent woman exercised a rather silly non-thought-out move and found herself bouncing across the asphalt of a four-lane road. YES! I attempted to scratch my right ear with my left hand while riding my scooter at 35 mph. All the questions you are asking yourself about that decision of mine, I already asked myself and I can save you some time and energy – there is no reasonable answer.

I lost control of the bike, wobbling for who knows how long trying to slow down while squeezing the accelerator instead of the brake. I landed in the opposing traffic lane where the scooter fell on top of my left foot whose shoe was attached to the rear wheel. People came to my side immediately from every direction. The bike was lifted carefully off my foot breaking my shoe which released my foot from the wheel. Folks lifted me out of the street and onto the grass. I remember reaching up to feel for my helmet which was securely in place. Thank goodness. A very nice woman named Cindy called all the appropriate rescue people and my cousin, Chris, whom I was visiting! I felt so grateful but couldn't say anything. I guess I was in shock.

Within moments, a fire truck and ambulance were on the scene. After answering a zillion questions and the paramedics had sliced up my jeans, I just laid back and breathed several deep breaths of extreme gratitude. I had no idea what was cut, bruised, or broken, but it didn't matter. I was alive, I could breathe, think, and speak and I was being well cared for by perfect strangers. My guardian angels had worked overtime on my behalf that day without a doubt. On the ride to the hospital, I was noticing that parts of my body were burning and other parts were throbbing. All I could do during that time was to breathe slowly and deliberately.

My entire ER experience was as good as it gets, I'm thinking. All those attending to my needs were kind, efficient, knowledgeable, and humorous. They provided a much-needed levity without disregarding the painful reality. When the attendant snipped off the final threads to remove my jeans, he apologized for having to throw them away. I said, "No problem, they were on their last leg anyway!" The registration nurse and the attendant laughed hysterically! The craziest part was that I hadn't realized I made a "funny" until the nurse slapped her hand on the counter and cracked up, repeating my words!

After the results of the twelve x-rays were in, the doctor stopped by to explain the results. He said that at my age and given the conditions of the accident, having only four impressive road burns and only ONE broken bone, I was one lucky woman! Miraculous, to say the least! He went on to say that I had fractured my left heel bone, would be put in a splint for a week, then either a cast or a boot and be out of commission for eight to twelve weeks. My first reaction to the news was one of extremely mixed emotions, mostly gratitude and devastation! A weird combination, huh?

My cousin Chris and his wife Carol arrived at the hospital after they went to the scene and recovered my scooter and helmet. That was only the beginning of a week's worth of loving care they graciously provided, which included helping me keep things light. On Friday, I had my appointment with the orthopedic surgeon. Then on Saturday my cousin and his wife drove Van-Go and me to my friend Marie's who lived four hours away!

All things considered; the entire incident was a temporary inconvenience at best! Besides, I would be recuperating at Marie's place in Madeira Beach, Florida, exactly one block from the beach. So, really, how bad could that be? An amazing element was that Marie just moved there three weeks earlier! Had she not been there and welcomed me to stay with her until my foot was completely healed, I would have had to fly back to Maryland and stay with family there. I will forever and sincerely be in her debt.

Judi Ronco

Life in the Boot

Now that I was in a permanent place to recoup from the accident, Marie and I got busy making adjustments for her having a temporarily incapacitated friend being there in a completely different way than we had planned. Plan A was for me to come for a couple weeks to hang out on the beach, head to the Everglades and have a blast in Key West making memories. Memories were made indeed, just of a different nature!

Marie was kind enough to prepare lovely meals and run around gathering things I needed. She assigned a reachable space in a cabinet for my kitchen needs right next to the fridge. As for me, I did discover how to do a few things on my own. I put my book, medication, water bottle and other small items in my cloth laptop case holding the handles with my right hand while also grasping the crutch...pretty ingenious, I thought! I even made breakfast twice. Her kitchen was perfectly sized and laid out for me to hobble about and lean when necessary.

Five days after I arrived at Marie's was my first follow up with the orthopedic surgeon. Everyone I dealt with was personable, funny, knowledgeable, and compassionate. Dr. Scott McGinley was great. He had me laughing after a few minutes of talking when he said, "I have a feeling that you're not going to be a well-behaved patient. My wife is Italian, too. Trust me, I speak from the voice of experience!"

He gave me the option of a boot or a cast. With a boot, I'd have to be off my foot entirely, I couldn't get it wet, I could remove it periodically to shower and to give my foot and leg some air. With a cast, I could walk as usual, I could get a little water on it as long as I dried it well, and I had to keep it on for at least four months.

"That's a no-brainer, Doc. I'll stay off my foot completely before I feel trapped in a cast. What if I would have an itch?"

86

He laughed. "A boot it is then." He called for Lisa, who would fit me for the boot. I was surprised when she walked through the door. She was also wearing a boot, the perfect person to give me the inside scoop on how to navigate with this new contraption.

Then Jennifer came in to officially check me out because I wouldn't be going back to that office from then on because it was too far away. She had a very rough morning in the office. She was pregnant with her second child and was exhausted all the time. Her other child was eight years old and as active as they come. We laughed a lot about kids and my crazy accident. She even thanked me for cheering her up. Go figure.

Back at Marie's, online ordering of a tub seat, handrail, extended shower head and a knee walker became a priority. I wasn't thrilled with the new showering requirements especially having to take the boot off beforehand and putting it back on after, but at least I *could* shower. Once I got the hang of the knee walker, it became a real blessing and almost fun except for when I ran into the baseboards several times. It got me off those awkward and uncomfortable crutches though.

A couple weeks later, Easter was upon us and Marie and her friend helped me to the beach. They lugged all the equipment and I lugged me. It was nothing short of a miracle! Walking on the beach on crutches was a hoot. A few specific movements were crucial to remaining in an upright position until I arrived at my spot!

1- Place each crutch, one at a time, into the sand as far as it will go
2- Make sure shoulders and hand grips are in place
3- Lean forward enough so you don't fall back
4- Lift and slide good foot forward, but not too far
5- Pay close attention to balance issues
6- Allow boo-boo foot to swing up to match good foot placement
7- Pull one crutch out of sand and move slightly forward
8- Pull second crutch out and move it forward
9- Repeat # 1 – 8 for every step you take!
10- Celebrate when you arrive in vertical mode!

It's amazing how much we take for granted when everything works on its own! I'll never take my mobility for granted again!

The ladies put the umbrella up during lunch to prevent the seagulls from grabbing our food right out of our hands. They were a bit aggressive there. For whatever reason, they won't swoop under an umbrella. Crazy birds!

When it was time to leave, Marie and her friend gathered all our goodies and started for the parking lot, glancing back to make sure I was okay. I got myself up out of the chair and began my journey back through the sand monster. Not five steps in, I heard a voice, "Miss, can I help you?"

I looked up and there stood a very tall sturdy young man with a pleasant smile. I laughed and said, "Only if you plan to carry me!" Very seriously, he replied that it was exactly what he had in mind. He told me to trust him and he handed my crutches off to a perfect stranger and asked him to follow us.

He placed one arm around my waist and had me wrap my arms around his neck and he scooped me up like I was a feather and carried me to the curb. In a moment of sincere gratitude, I boldly told him I loved him. He smiled and said, "Well, it was the least I could do considering all the rotten things I've done in my twenty-three years of life."

I assured him he had burned a lot of karma with this act of kindness. We both laughed heartily over that one. He retrieved my crutches from the friendly man who got volunteered to assist and waited with me until Marie brought the car around. Whatever anyone might call that event, I chose to call it a miracle!

Later, after we showered and rested up, Marie and I went to dinner. The restaurant had only second floor seating with access via a pyramid-high set of stairs. We looked at each other and shrugged our shoulders. As we turned to go back to the car, Marie noticed a sign, ELEVATOR! It was next to the handicapped parking area. Oh, yeah, another miracle. I was on a roll. In order for me to have a chair to prop my foot up on, the hostess seated us at a table for four, but it was in a high traffic area. Marie noticed a table in the corner overlooking the marina. A couple was just leaving from it. Marie asked if we could sit there instead. Wish granted AND we could hear the live music being played on the opposite deck. Yep! Another miracle! Three's a charm! We were both bursting with appreciation for the turn of events that day!

Another couple of weeks went by and for the most part, I had maintained a decent attitude since the accident. There was a week though, somewhere during the process, where my frame of mind was immensely erratic. It had been a long time since my emotions were riding the "roller coaster" like that week. I was grateful. I was angry. I was hopeful. I was sick of reading, then falling asleep. Nothing was on TV. I kept banging my foot into things. I was glad for ice packs. Food was boring! Every single thing I did required so much energy. Showers became a major ordeal. My entire functioning wardrobe consisted of a handful of sundresses. Even all my colored pencils began to look alike!

I was headed into an emotional pit and struggling to hold onto the surface! I was the hostess of my own pity party!

Marie suggested we go to an open-air market nearby. I begrudgingly set up my knee walker and went along. It was lovely. Beautiful fresh produce, tasters of preservative-free yummies, and several craft booths were there. The ground was rocky, so my movements were challenging, but I was starting to feel better. Tiring out quickly though, I asked if we could go back. It was definitely good to have a bit of relief from the funk I was in.

As I was hobbling into the house, Marie went to check the mail. I noticed a package sitting in front of the door with my name on it. I couldn't imagine what it could be. I got settled on the sofa and opened it almost furiously. It was filled with goodies from my daughter Rachel and her wife Megan. Wrapped in different colored tissue paper were five smaller packages. Craft items, a tear-jerker movie, a Family Feud card game, Nutter Butter peanut butter sandwich cookies, and a sweet greeting card. I cried a happy cry for the first time in quite a while. How thoughtful were they? They sure knew me well. My heart was beating fast with joy and thankfulness. Funny how something outside yourself will come along to help you shift your perspective when it doesn't bubble up from within. Life is good.

Three weeks later, I received a promising report from the orthopedist. My foot was healing well and the bone had stayed in the perfect position for bonding. I learned that the calcaneus or heel bone connects with other bones and that joint is important for normal foot function. It didn't break apart, just split. That was the good news. What threw me was the timeline for proper healing. Two more months with the boot with zero pressure on the foot, then about six weeks to get the whole walking thing down again. That entailed walking on the boot in the house at least a week, walking on the sidewalk with the boot, walking in the house with a shoe then walking outside with a shoe. Only then would I be released to continue my sorely missed Van-Go Adventure! Finally, I would be instructed to follow a limited physical activity plan for at least another seven months. Of course, I had quite an abbreviated timeline in mind for that last segment of recuperation! I was up and running, well walking – more like shuffling in four months just in time for my son's wedding in October.

Due to the time crunch, my plans to drive to Maryland included only enough time at campgrounds to sleep and get off my feet. I discovered that more patience and commitment were necessary to allow complete healing and range of motion to return to my foot than I could have possibly imagined. The words of the orthopedic surgeon kept ringing in my head, "If you do this now, it will pay off later." He was right, but boy was it torturous in the meantime. Two things kept me going more often than not.

One was truly feeling grateful for my life that could have been lost that day. The second was placing my hand across my chest to feel the beating of my own heart.

A Visit from the Heart

Toward the end of my fourth month of recuperation, my daughter Rachel and her wife Megan flew from Maryland to Madeira Beach, Florida, to visit and see how I was doing. Their loving gesture was entirely unexpected. It did my heart good to see their cheerful faces. We hung out for the better part of five days. Knowing how virtually impossible it was for me to get to the beach myself, they made it their mission to make sure I would experience as much beach time as possible while they were there. Mission accomplished!

Marie had taken a job that required her to travel, so I had been on my own for about two months. I hadn't been near the water because it was too difficult of a walk and I didn't want to risk it alone. My "angels" walked me to the beach with each of them holding onto one of my crutches and me. Even with a few close calls, we made it. Off we went to what seemed like miles to the shoreline. They rented an inner tube for me to sit on and attempted to place me on an outer rim. That lasted about twenty seconds. A wave came and into the center hole I went. Our laughter stretched far beyond the small area we occupied, and we had piggyback chucklers on either side of us. The girls and I played in the water for hours enjoying every second of it. When we finished playing, we managed to dry me off and get me back to the house. For the next several days, we hobbled to the beach together, talked and laughed, ate beachy foods, and sunned ourselves until we couldn't stand it anymore.

It has been five years since that beautiful surprise visit and I'm as grateful for it now as I was then. We still talk about it and how family is a precious gift of love, support, compassion, and laughter all rolled into one. I've been gifted with children who are not only great kids but incredible people. One of the greatest aspects of having grown children is the friendship that evolves with time. This visit was just one example of their commitment to our family friendship. My three children are close and they're always there for each other. With me being gone for nearly eight years including my four years living in New Mexico, my wonderful sister, Tanya, kept a watchful eye on them. I will be grateful to her forever for such a loving gesture. She also created a tradition of having Thanksgiving breakfast at her house that continues to this day. She was there for them when I couldn't be and they were there for her as well.

Families are worth the ups and downs, moments of misunderstanding, and occasional personality clashes because the bottom line is that the love among its members is stronger than any temporary uncomfortable situation. I've been blessed with family that I would have chosen as friends if they weren't given to me!

Back in Action: On the Road Again

Once I was officially released by my orthopedic surgeon to travel, as I mentioned earlier, I streamlined my trip back to Maryland for my son's wedding. Nonetheless, my gift of sharing precious time with folks who knew the joy in feeling good and being grateful continued.

Three especially marvelous encounters that stuck with me I have chosen to share here.

Moment with a Fisherman: Between Georgia and Alabama I spent a night at a Camping World, then onto Hidden Cove Resort the next morning for a few days. The highlight of the beautiful property was their lake. Houses were situated along the shoreline and resembled what you might see on a postcard. Each cottage-like home had a boat slip jutting out into the crystal-clear lake. There was a long winding pathway down to the lake and a large, covered deck with picnic tables overlooking the water. At the base of the stairs were huge flat boulders where I could be found early in the mornings waiting patiently to welcome the sun. I have always been drawn to sunrises. Each one brings the wonder of a new day with endless possibilities. The sun appears in all her glory to greet its onlookers. The first morning that I went to the river, a man came along with his fishing pole. We exchanged "good mornings" and I commented on the dense fog before us and he replied in a soft and gentle voice, "Yes, it truly adds a sense of mystery to the lake. I've lived here all my life and I never tire of its magic." I smiled at him. That simple remark felt as if it rose up from his heart. It sparked a sense of wonder and appreciation in mine for my life as a whole, the beauty of nature, and for the opportunity I have every day to recognize each moment as a blessing. That brief encounter with a stranger heightened my awareness and revived my connection to all things. Though I didn't get his name, I felt like I knew him somehow even for a moment. I often wished that I would have acknowledged him for touching my life in such a sweet way. Perhaps he felt it in my smile.

Grandma Extraordinaire: At a small diner on my way out of town, I had the pleasure of meeting a woman named Robbie. She wore a nurse's uniform and appeared exhausted. She must have just come off her shift. She sat at a booth sipping coffee with her eyes focused downward. As I was leaving the diner, I walked to her booth and wished her a lovely day. Her reply surprised me.

"It's always a good day with my two darling granddaughters." She continued fluently as if she wanted someone to hear her story. "The first little angel came to me at eight months and the second at ten months." She asked if I had a few minutes. I sat down across from her. As her story unfolded, she revealed that both of her daughters had severe drug addictions. Robbie agreed to take care of the children until their mothers were released from the rehabilitation facility. They were released two years later and Grandma still had the girls. The temporary situation became permanent.

"I now find myself at age fifty, thinking about schools, doctor visits, proper nutrition and potty training. They're the loves of my life. I chose to adopt them and continue to raise them in the absence of their birth mothers, my daughters. I'm saddened that my girls will miss out on an opportunity that could have filled their lives with purpose." Robbie blotted her eyes.

I thanked her for her act of love and told her that she would surely reap the benefits of her altruistic choice and wished her all the joy that was possible during her journey. I rested my hand on hers for a couple minutes before I went on my way.

I pondered how common that type of scenario probably is in these times and if you know someone who is raising or has raised the children of others, please thank them if possible and send wishes that they might find joy in their loving gesture.

Got Pizza? As I continued to travel north, I got the kind of hankering for an amazing pizza that one might get for a sip of water while crawling through the desert! So, I went Google crazy searching for a five-star pizza joint on my way.

One place kept popping up but was a half hour away and slightly off course. I didn't care. I was willing to risk it. It was worth it with every bite. My Mediterranean pizza with mushrooms and onions added was a culinary delight. My mouth waters now just recalling the experience. When my server came by to ask how the pizza was, I raved about it without hesitation. I had to ask who made it and how long they have been creating these spectacular pizzas. He satisfied my curiosity.

"Well, first, all our ingredients are made in house. I'm Johnny and I have known Vinnie, the owner here at Palermo's Pizza Grill and Catering for six years. Prior to that I was taught by my dad, who also owned a pizza parlor, since I was a little guy. First, I got to watch, then wash dishes, and finally at age ten, I got to make the dough. My Papa always said, 'The dough, Johnny, it's the most important part of a great pizza.'" He also told me that he loved coming to work every day because it reminded him of those years he cherished with his father.

I thanked him for sharing his story and left a note on my check for Vinnie, "Continued good luck with your business and hold onto Johnny. He's a gem."

Some people were meant to make a specific contribution to this life and Johnny was born to make sensational pizza. From anyone who has been delighted with his destiny, we say a hearty "Thank you!"

Reflections

When a life-altering incident occurs that brings with it the potential for unwanted change, the search for an uplifting thought is crucial. Finding a way to feel good about such an incident can make all the difference in your recovery process. It certainly did for me. You can fight it or accept it and see the wisdom wrapped up in it. Taking your mind from "poor me" to "fortunate me" will allow an opening in your heart for gratitude.

In my case, just to be alive was a good enough feel-good thought for me. I still think about how if one single piece of the picture had been different, I may not have been here to write about it. Even though the accident altered my dream adventure by several months, I decided to discover different kinds of adventures that I could experience and feel good about. The more I accepted my situation, the lighter I felt and the more things happened that eased the recuperation "drama." I gave it my all to focus on what I did have rather than what I was being deprived of especially when the disappointment and frustration reared their ugly heads. It took a tremendous conscious effort on my part many times. I'm here to tell you, it wasn't always easy, but it was absolutely worth it. I'm a better woman for having chosen the kinds of thoughts and feelings I did over the ones that I could have been thinking and feeling.

Feeling good is paramount in every regard! It gets easier with each choice to seek out a reason to smile.

> *"Some days there won't be a song in your heart. Sing anyway."*
>
> — EMORY AUSTIN

> *"To be upset over what you don't have is to waste what you DO have."*
>
> — KEN S. KEYES, JR.

Chapter 6 – In Service

Not an Average Gesture of Kindness

I love life's little surprises! Heck, I love life's BIG surprises, especially when they're wrapped in kindness.

Still on crutches, but kickin' butt with my mobility, I was out one day "running" errands. I spent forty-five minutes at the post office during Mother's Day season waiting to send off a package to my daughter. Trudging along, I stopped at a fabric store for some thread to affix a button. It was 1:45 p.m. and my next stop would have been Walmart for groceries. My growling belly suggested I eat decent food first before I entered the hub of temptation on an empty stomach. Go, belly!

Texas Roadhouse was in the same parking lot as the Walmart. I parked close to the entrance, grabbed my crutches, and made a futile attempt to open the door. It was locked! I stood there bewildered for a moment, then a genuinely nice man showed me to another door with a bell on the side. He pushed it and told me to have a seat on the bench and wait. I complied mostly out of curiosity even though I was confused.

A few minutes later, to my delight, a handsome young man opened the door and said, "My, my, what do we have here? Can I help you?"

"Well, actually, I'd like to come in and have some lunch."

He smiled apologetically and told me they didn't open until 4:00 p.m. I was so bummed. I said okay and was getting ready to leave, contemplating Plan B. I turned toward the parking lot and heard him call out to me, "Wait a minute. If you don't mind not actually having a server, I would be happy to fix you a delicious salad and check on you myself."

If that wasn't an offer I couldn't refuse, I never heard one! I hobbled through the open door and followed him to a seat. I got comfy with my foot elevated on a chair across from me and ordered a Caesar salad. Moments later, Trevor delivered my lunch. As it turned out, he was the proprietor of the restaurant. I thanked him and told him to go in the back and do whatever he needed to do because I was perfectly fine. I had the entire air-conditioned place to myself, great music to listen to and was being tended to by the owner. How much better could it get?

The third time he checked on me I was finished and I felt compelled to tell him about my Bright Spots since he was certainly one in MY day. He blushed. Then he said, "I actually have something I could share that I consider happy news in my life."

He didn't have to twist my arm. I asked if he had time to sit with me so I could jot it down. He said he'd be happy to. "You see, I recently took over this restaurant. Real recently, like last Wednesday and it was also my birthday. I was with another restaurant for twelve years but chose to join the Texas Roadhouse team because of their philosophy. This company sees the customer as their highest priority."

"I certainly felt that today with your 'over the top' hospitality." He nodded.

He explained that Texas Roadhouse doesn't spend money on advertising. They get the word out about their restaurant through their "legendary store marketers." Carol is theirs. She's employed forty hours a week to engage in community outreach. She goes everywhere giving out coupons, appetizers, other sample menu items, telling folks first-hand about the restaurant. Carol is also instrumental in raising money for various charities through the restaurant. When he became aware of this concept, he knew he wanted to be a part of it. He quit his other job and bought this Texas Roadhouse location. It had only been six days, but so far, so good.

I thanked him for an amazing story and his kindness. I let him know how grateful I was that I was hungry when he was around. We laughed.

I was ready to give him my credit card and he placed his hand over mine. "This one's on me. And just for the record, the real shining lights in my life each and every day are my wife and my two little guys. Our oldest is three and the newest member is eleven months." The gentle expression in his eyes as he told me about his family suggested to me that Trevor was probably a man filled with love and integrity that spread across all aspects of his life. That thought warmed my heart. I smiled, thanking him again as he helped me up and walked me to the door.

Best Tour Guide Ever

After a long drive, I arrived late and in the dark at the campground. Fortunately, a kind woman welcomed me at the entrance to give me my camper's packet. I woke up after a great night's sleep to find my van surrounded by bunnies. When I went up to the office to pay for my site, the cashier asked me, "Would you believe that two years ago, there were only five rabbits? Now, the campground has become somewhat of a sanctuary for the masses!" We laughed and laughed.

As I was strolling through the grounds, a young boy happened by on his bike. We immediately began chatting about many things. We talked about the "bunny takeover" first as it was front and center as well as behind and beside us! Then he asked me if I wanted to see something awesome. "Absolutely, what is it?"

"Oh, just follow me on my bike. I'll go slow."

I walked fast and he rode slowly so we could continue our chat on the way to our destination, which turned out to be a waterfall and a little beach area. It was so cute and cozy. The falls were all of four feet high and the beach about the size of a small kitchen. I was thrilled. It was perfect. There, as I sat on the rocks, Jackson, age eleven, told me about his dream while he was climbing in and around the water. He wanted to become a paleontologist.

"I study snakes, you know. They're so awesome and stuff. Every time I see one, I wonder where it came from and how long it's been around. I think some creatures are the same ones from the dinosaur times. Not the same, same, but turned into other things that started a really long time ago. I'm in middle school and I'm really good at Math. I'll have to go to college to learn a lot more, but that's cool."

After we hung out there awhile, he extended my tour of the grounds which included the pool. It was a large concrete five-foot deep empty hole except for a few leaves. Being just after Labor Day, Jackson suggested I come back during the summer because it was a lot of fun. It was getting close to lunchtime, and Jackson needed to check in with his mom and dad. I followed him to their camp site only to find that it was right next to mine! He went inside and I headed to the office to purchase bunny food for us to feed the multitudes of fluffy little cotton-tails. By the time I got back, Jackson had eaten and was anxious to play. We had a blast with the bunnies. They were all over us, climbing on our legs as we sat on the ground. They stumbled all over each other trying to get to the pellets. We laughed so hard our bellies ached. My favorite bunny, if I had to choose, was a tiny one with one lop ear that was the only brown spot on his otherwise pure white body. It looked like his ear had been dipped in chocolate!

Jackson saw his mom come outside and he asked me to go say hello. I walked over with him and introduced myself. I told her I was in the van next to her. I explained how Jackson had been a polite, funny, and all-around wonderful tour guide showing me the campground.

She was pleased and shared that Jackson was quite the talker and interested in everything especially meeting new people. She told me he has been homeschooled since kindergarten, but he would be off to a regular high school in a couple years. "He has big plans, and he'll need the right kind of schooling."

I thanked her for sharing her delightful son with me and what a pleasure it was spending time with him. I said good-bye and thanked Jackson for a fun and informative day. I left him with a couple bags of bunny food for the next day. He reached out to shake my hand and I obliged.

I went into Van-Go and fixed lunch, thinking how fortunate I was to run into Jackson. At only eleven years old, he reminded me in his own subtle way about reasons to be happy like family, fun, helping others, and having a dream. What a kid!

Sharing the Wealth

Two curious young men were spotted peering into my van windows as I was returning from a stroll through St. Joseph, Michigan. It wasn't the first such sighting that I witnessed. Calling to them, nearly scaring the bajeebies out of them, made me laugh. They had that deer-in-the-headlights look on their faces. I let them know they weren't in trouble and if they would like to see the inside of Van-Go, I could arrange it since she belonged to me. They jumped at the opportunity. They were both about five foot nine, which left them hunched over as they entered the van. I told them to sit on the sofa while I popped the top, allowing a seven-foot standing space. They were absolutely flabbergasted. We sat and talked about all the quotes on the outside of the van and how they would like to meet the person who did such an awesome job decorating my van. Wish granted! I raised my hand.

As I shared about my adventure, I noticed they both had a few t-shirts slung over their forearms. I paused to ask about them. When Parker began to explain with such passion and animation, I asked him if he would mind writing their story down in my Bright Spots notebook so I didn't miss a thing. He agreed and handed his shirts to his friend. What follows are Parker's words verbatim.

"We love giving back to the people and seeing the happiness spread. Spending our time down here on the beaches in downtown St. Joe is what us kids do here in these parts. It's great to see all the smiles from people either just swinging through or the ones that lived here their whole lives. A few of us have started a brand called, Straight Bummin'. We make tie-dye shirts, tank tops, bucket hats, and sunglasses. Fifty percent of all our profits go to the United Way and local charities. It's a great thing to see something you created yourself blossom and help people in a cool new way! Happiness by any means necessary! If you're looking for a safe and fun time with some good vibes, swing on through St. Joe, Michigan's Silver Beach and enjoy yourself."

I was quite impressed with these two boys and told them how refreshing it was to meet young people with a vision for the betterment of all and getting in there and making it happen. They were providing a service and having fun doing it. So cool! I gave a contribution to their cause and wished them the greatest success with their project!

The following day I took their lead and ventured to Silver Beach. It was clean and the waves were gentle as they rolled into shore. My plan for spending the day sunning myself morphed into a three-hour walking tour. It was a blast. I saw lighthouses and wineries and went into the Olive Cart where you can taste a plethora of extra virgin olive oils and aged balsamic vinegars. To add to the adventure of culinary ecstasy, I indulged in tasters of glazes, stuffed olives, and freshly baked breads. I could have spent the day in there. Next, I stopped in the Fuzzy Butz Pet Bakery where I purchased a few gourmet treats for my own kids' pups. The final place I ventured into was the Box Factory for the Arts. It housed a wide array of eclectic art and special areas where the public could observe an artist at work and ask questions about their craft.

One of my two favorite sites that kept a smile on my face the rest of the day was the St. Joe Carousel with its gorgeous old-fashioned décor in all its splendor. The horses, giraffes, zebras, and high-backed wooden benches were alive with an array of colors and trimmed in gold. Most of the animals effortlessly raised and lowered as the music and whirling lights captured my attention. Painted panels depicting past and present scenes of the area wrapped around the center of the carousel. I rode round and round in childlike awe.

The other was the Whirlpool Compass Fountain that squirted water up like rockets out of holes in the concrete totally at random. There were tall ones, short ones and combinations of the two. I discovered it was referred to as a splash pad. It was the perfect end to a perfect day to run through not knowing when you would get cooled off by one or more of the jets of water flying in the air. There was so much more to see. I couldn't take it all in in one afternoon though. I had enough fun to last me for days! It was like being a kid again. I was grateful for a second time to the "t-shirt" boys!

Like My Own

Home Depot became more than a "fix-it" store for me one day. While I was there searching for the camping department, a gentleman offered to assist me. We found what I needed. I told him about my journey and we got to talking about kids, family, retirement, and more. Brian worked at Home Depot several days a week, but his full-time job and passion for the past thirty-five years was as a research chemist at Aberdeen Proving Grounds in Maryland. I asked if he had thought about retirement anytime soon. He remarked that he loved his job and would continue to work until he just couldn't do it anymore! Another passion of his was his involvement with elder care. I shared that I admired him for doing that type of volunteerism. "I certainly benefit much more from the experience of being with that wise and loving population than I could possibly be giving to them." I smiled.

Brian admitted that the aspect of his life that he cherished the most was the love, respect, and pride he has for his two biological daughters and what he refers to as his two "spiritual" daughters. Deborah-twenty-five, Abigail-sixteen, Kristina-twenty-five, and Victoria-sixteen are great joys in his life. When I asked about his "spiritual" daughters, he explained that he met them through his church and has mentored them for many years. He spoke of the four of them as peas in a pod and feels honored to have them in his life. My conversation with Brian lit up my day and it was wonderful to spend a brief time with a man who spreads his light so graciously in so many ways.

All About the Kids

Feeling grateful that I always carry a pad and pencil in my backpack, I chuckled as I grabbed them both and quickly walked over to where I overheard a man talking about what sounded like a feel-good story. I approached him asking if he had a few minutes to share more about the event. I told him I was traveling and collecting great stories along my journey. He was more than happy to roll with it. The gentleman was Superintendent Mark R. He explained that the park's third annual Outdoor Educational Rendezvous, offered free of charge to children and adults alike, was coming up in a few days. This program provided an opportunity for the participants to learn about the great outdoors firsthand from trained instructors and naturalists. In years past, over 500 students took advantage of this program and swarmed to the park on the special day.

The instructors shared information verbally, showed slide and video presentations, and most importantly, allowed the children to actively engage in many activities. A variety of topics were explored. They actually fished while learning the types of fish indigenous to the area. They heard about eagle nesting and facts specific to the raptors. The children learned about the characteristics of the wetlands which include marshes, lakes, rivers, and forested swamps. They learned that the wetlands provide food, covering, and nesting grounds for wildlife such as birds, butterflies, ducks, and geese. The visitors were invited to tour the wetlands and see for themselves the interesting facts that were shared. Archery was also among the activities for the day. Of course, pony rides, sticking hands into fish tanks and eating s'mores could certainly not be overlooked as additional ways of having fun at that event.

I thanked Mark. I thoroughly enjoyed listening to him as he described the event. His warm smile, his animated delivery and his bright eyes were all clear indicators of what he actually told me at the end of our chat, "You know, ma'am, I look forward to this day with a sense of pride, accomplishment, and joy. I love nature and I love the kids' innate curiosity about the 'great outdoors'

105

and what it has to offer." It was a pleasant surprise to have had the good fortune to speak with Superintendent Mark, who provides such a beneficial and memorable opportunity to the public. Even more important was that he absolutely loved being part of it. Kudos to him and his staff.

I'm thrilled that I am able to share these stories of goodwill and love throughout my journey.

Disaster Turns to Treasure

I had the opportunity to walk through several Gulf towns that were part of the Hurricane Katrina devastation of August 2005. Even though New Orleans, Louisiana was the "hardest hit," life in southern Mississippi was also disrupted substantially, requiring its residents to rebuild their homes and businesses. It was difficult to imagine what it must have been like to see your "life" in total shambles. My heart ached for them as I sat on a bench envisioning the ramifications of such devastation, not so much physical but emotional. Once I gathered my own feelings of compassion, I noticed several amazing sculptures along the roadway. I wanted to know more about them, so I found the Chamber of Commerce building and discovered their remarkable story.

One man who had experienced a few years back, the camaraderie that occurs when disaster strikes, chose to help beautify what was once a spectacle of destruction. Marlin Miller, an award-winning "wood sculptor" from Fort Walton Beach, Florida was inspired by the works of art along Beach Boulevard in Biloxi created by the internationally award-winning "chainsaw artist," Dayton Scoggins. Scoggins had carved sea creatures out of topped off trees damaged by the storm. Miller approached the city about donating his time and talent to sculpt additional trees. He explained that he wanted to return the favor to the residents of Biloxi who helped his community recover from Hurricane Ivan a few years prior. Over the course of several years, he created fifteen works of art. What an exceptional way to pay it forward where so many people can appreciate not only his skill as a chainsaw sculptor, but to reminisce how communities assist each other in times of need and feel a sense of pride. You can Google "Hurricane Katrina Tree Sculptures" to see all the carvings as of October 2020, including the marine-related objects that Dayle Lewis of Indiana contributed since I was there. The tree-sculptures are located all along scenic Highway 90. There are now approximately fifty sculptures throughout the Mississippi Gulf Coast. Included is the world's largest eagle sculpture, standing seventeen feet tall and located in War Memorial Park on Highway 90 in Pass Christian!

When I was walking along Highway 95, able to stand close to each carving, seeing, and touching the details, I could almost feel the love and appreciation that went into each masterpiece. The time and talent that went into creating these structures, for me, was secondary to the desire to give back and serve the people of the Mississippi Gulf Coast. What a gift the communities received from these compassionate artists!

One Hundred Fifty Guests for Thanksgiving Dinner?

While in Pensacola, I went to the National Naval Aviation Museum to see the Blue Angel planes because the pilots train there and I always thought their air tricks were amazing. I left with a whole new respect and compassion for families of wartime. Observing the models of ships and planes, reading about their contribution to various wars, viewing pictures of those who served during wartime, and of wreckages found on the floor of Lake Michigan, somehow shifted me inside.

I never appreciated history of any kind in school. I found it boring and unnecessary. It certainly had no relevance to me. I was humbled by my visit to this museum and felt a bit ashamed about my lack of interest throughout my life. Perhaps I've taken for granted the fact that during my lifetime I haven't experienced the fear of sending a child away not knowing if they would return alive or the loss of everything familiar because of continuous bombings. I didn't relate my safe life to the sacrifice of thousands of men and women who risked theirs. Even though I have no firsthand experience with what so many families had to bear, my heart is now open to them and their courage and loyalty. With much respect, admiration, and appreciation, I say, "Thank you."

Thanksgiving Eve, I joined some of the campers at a community fire. We were chatting about the ins and outs of the RV life. Then we shared what we were going to contribute to the Thanksgiving dinner at the campground. One woman said she was hoping that ninety-six deviled eggs were going to be enough. My eyes widened. I asked who in the world was going to eat all those eggs especially since the owners were supplying the main dishes? As it turned out, there would be approximately 150 people there on Thursday, about forty of which would be young military men and women! The campground owners were bussing them in from the naval base. Most of the young men and women would be experiencing their first Thanksgiving away from home. Apparently, the campground had been sponsoring this event each of the six years they had been in business! I was so touched by this immense gesture of love and respect. The owners were supplying nine turkeys, hams, fresh local oysters, pies, and so much more. Campers were going all out for this celebration. I told them they could count me in! I chose to make mini skewers with heart shaped strawberries, mini marshmallows, and blueberries (red, white, and blue) for everyone! This Thanksgiving meal was going to be an opportunity for me to say thank you in person and be part of a beautiful community effort to help those young Marines feel at home. I was so honored that I would be there for the next day's heartwarming event.

A Few Words from the Marines on Thanksgiving

The young Marines took time out on that blessed day to join us at Pensacola RV Park in a celebration of gratitude. After the drill sergeant spoke to the group just off the bus about the day's schedule, dinner was served cafeteria-style and folks scattered about finding a spot to enjoy the feast.

The sun was shining much of the day, but it got chilly later beckoning for a community campfire. Navigating from one Marine to another, I had the distinct pleasure of chatting with several of them after dinner. Each one with whom I spent time warmed my heart. Their honesty, enthusiasm, dedication, and gratitude expressed for being invited there and for life itself delighted me! I felt honored to have had that time with them. The following accounts were shared with me as we sat around the campfire.

Zachary was from Detroit, Michigan, and had always wanted to be a Marine. His field of interest was aviation mechanics. "Every day that I wake up is a reason to be happy."

Alan was from Manassas, Virginia, and his area of specialty was aviation support. He would be learning about every trade in aviation so he can pitch in whenever needed! "Being so far from home, it means the world to me that I'm able to still stay in touch with my family."

Julie was from Massachusetts, and the first in her family to serve in the military. She chose this path for the adventure, the travel, and the challenge. She had been in the service nine months and was training in the field of aviation electronics because it would serve her well in the civilian world as well. "I wake up every morning proud to be a Marine, Ms. Judi."

There was a slight pause in the sharing. Chavis, one of the Marines, was about to experience his first s'more. A group chanted, "On your mark, get set, go!" He did it! But did he like it?

"I don't think I have ever tasted that combination of foods before. I think it was...different."

Those of us watching that monumental event could hardly stop laughing.

Back to the Marines...

Thomas and Jonathan were in the same platoon and very grateful to be at the celebration that day because last year on Thanksgiving they were in boot camp! "This is heaven compared to boot camp," said Thomas. "Anything is better than boot camp," Jonathan chimed in. More laughter all around.

Sam had been in the marines for nine months and shared confidently and enthusiastically that it had been the best decision he ever made. He was from Florida and a year ago found himself with little money working at the Waffle House. A Marine recruiter came into the restaurant one day and the rest is history! "I'll always remember the look of pride on my parents' faces when I graduated from boot camp this past summer on Friday, June 13, 2014. I'll never forget that day."

Jordan, from Texas, had been in the marines sixteen months and would soon be driving across the country from Ohio to his duty station in Miramar, California, to begin work with aviation electronics. He had recently gotten engaged and set the date for June 8, 2015. Congrats!

Austin was from Wisconsin, and it had been fourteen months since he joined the Marines. His field was also aviation electronics and he was grateful to have Jordan sharing in the cross-country adventure.

Michael joined the Marines fifteen months ago and was from Florida. He was extremely excited about getting the exact job that he wanted as a meteorological technician. To be working on weather forecasting equipment was a thrilling thought for him. Even with a seventy-five percent college scholarship available to him, Michael chose the Marines. "I'm mostly grateful that I'll be home for Christmas!"

Holden had been in the Marines for fourteen months and was from Utah. He was also assigned to work on weather equipment. He told me it was the rarest job in the entire Marine Corp. with only forty positions. He would be working out of South Carolina. When I asked why he joined the Marines, he replied, "I was headed in a direction destined to be harmful to myself and others, and that wasn't what I wanted for my life." Holden was born into a family of privilege and wanted to be his own man, do his own thing, work for what he achieved and become more independent. "One more special thing, I'm grateful that no distance can sever the ties and support of my family!"

It was a once in a lifetime opportunity for me to see into the hearts of those Marines and express my gratitude for their selfless choices to serve.

Reflections

Whichever end of a provided service you find yourself, you win! Doing for others is always a feel-good and uplifting endeavor. Having someone be kind, helpful, or respectful toward you has a way of making you feel great and making them feel great for providing an act that serves. Appreciation for a deed performed to improve the life or situation of a fellow human being must never go unnoticed. When you are able to recognize that win-win situation, that, in itself, will serve you well in uplifting your spirit.

Being in service is like being courageous in one very important way. Neither requires you to perform an extraordinarily over the top act. It's the common ordinary things you can do to serve or assist another. Any means of providing a service will undoubtedly leave you feeling good as long as it's done with love and authenticity. Being friendly to someone having a rough day, saying thank you to a person who completed a job well done, helping a child with their homework, listening to a friend's problem without judgment or picking up your trash after a picnic on the beach are all bite-sized yet important ways you can be of service.

*"Always render more and better service than is expected
by you, no matter what your task may be."*

— OG MANDINO

*"If you light a lamp for someone else, it will also brighten
your path."*

— BUDDHA

Chapter 7 – Future Vision - Dreams

Holding On to the Dream

While traveling through Texas, I had the most spectacular tour of a castle. It actually had a moat completely surrounding it. The only way to gain access to this fairy-tale structure was by walking across the three-thousand-pound drawbridge operated solely by a human "hamster wheel." It was surreal!

Let me start at the beginning. Over two decades ago, a man named Mike Newman started what's now an award-winning bakery nestled in the small town of Bellville. They open at 4:00 a.m. seven days a week. You could bask in the blend of aromas from their cinnamon buns, donuts, quiche, pigs in a blanket, and many other tasty treats before you even got inside the door. Some visitors were there simply to enjoy the treasures offered for breakfast or lunch. Others, like myself, gathered at the bakery while waiting for the castle tour guide. From there all ticket holders would follow the guide to the castle grounds located about five miles down the road. I couldn't speak for anyone else, but I was as excited as a child on Christmas morning.

Once all the tourists were parked and assembled outside the castle at the drawbridge, the gentleman who led the caravan instructed us to wait and our tour guide would be along momentarily. Hmm, I had thought he was our tour guide. About five minutes later, a gentleman dressed in Medieval-period clothing appeared, announcing himself as Mike Newman, the architect, builder, and resident of the castle! *The bakery guy?* I was stunned.

He welcomed everyone and began to tell us how the castle came to be. I think my mouth was still hanging open. First, in his early twenties, while touring Europe, he visited many castles hundreds of years old. He imagined what it would be like living in a castle. He dreamed for years of building a castle to live in. Then, at one point, figuring it was just a pipedream, he down-sized his vision to building a log cabin on the piece of property he bought in the countryside about five miles away from his bakery. After much deliberation with his friend and architect, he still wasn't sure about the "look" he was after. His friend said something to him that set into motion a plan that took eight years to complete.

"You know, Mike, you can have it look any way you want. After all, a man's home is his castle."

Mike told us he became flooded with memories of his ultimate dream of living in a real castle. Within days, the project of a lifetime had commenced. He admitted that he could hardly believe the wild endeavor he was about to undertake. Mike and one contractor broke ground in 1998 and built his castle one cinder block at a time. Even with it being over a decade later, I could feel the anticipation growing in his voice and the light in his eyes brightening as he continued. Each block brought on a new sense of wonder and joy for both men.

Once his castle was completed, he lived in it for several years with his immense and muscular dog Avalon, an Irish wolfhound. Mike was constantly sought after to be interviewed about his impressive residence as folks got wind of his masterpiece. He told the Texas Life magazine reporter, "In the beginning, people thought I was crazy; now, ten years later, I'm the king of my own castle."

Finally, he opened his home to the public after having added several sections that he rents out for special occasions. He gives every tour himself for $15. That includes his full story, castle-fun activities, a catapult demonstration, a complete lunch from his bakery, and the opportunity to do a self-guided tour of every single room, even his private quarters. Visitors were invited to walk the grounds at their own pace for as long as it was daylight. Avalon, ironically, was soon promoted to the honorary position of castle guard dog and greeter. Greeter, yes, but guard dog, not so much. Irish wolfhounds are known as gentle giants reaching up to three feet at their shoulders. Their size may ward off intruders, but certainly not their temperament!

Some exceptional features of the "king's" castle were his private chapel inside (it was blocked off from entry, but visitors could see most of it from behind the ropes), the cows that roamed freely about the grounds, the view from the turrets, and the fact that he built all the furniture. It even smelled like what I imagined an authentic Irish castle would have smelled like, kind of woodsy. The visitors were told they could join him in the dining room to eat anytime between noon and 2:00 p.m., so folks came and went. The main table sat thirty people! Mike himself served our bag lunches prepared at his bakery complete with a sweet treat. He even served up his homemade iced tea and spoke to people briefly as he refilled their cups.

It was an experience of a lifetime for me, especially since I was fortunate enough to spend a little more time with him later that day. I asked why he opened his home to the public, other than having been hounded by the press and community to do so. Mike replied that at first those were the primary reasons, then seeing the visitors' reactions and hearing their comments, he began to cherish having strangers fill his home during the tours. He shared his impression that it made people happy. They left with a restored faith that they could do anything.

He was so hospitable and unpretentious. I thanked him for his kindness and time and shook his hand that he extended to me. After all, he was just a man who had a dream that he made come true. So many of us have the dream and fail to recognize that we can make it come true. Just a shift in our thinking and a little courage to step out of our comfort zone can go a long way. What a privilege to meet someone who saw the possibilities for his life!

Be the Change

Who knew I would find a Bright Spot while searching for colored paper clips and Post-It notes in Office Max one afternoon? A young man, maybe twenty-two or so, came to my rescue asking if he could help me as I wandered throughout the aisles. I must have looked like a child lost in a corn maze at a county fair! We found what I needed and suddenly we were engaged in a wonderful conversation. He had asked me what I was planning to do with my newfound treasures, and I explained my project idea and about Van-Go and my adventure.

I think I hit a "happy" nerve because he opened up like a Morning Glory at dawn about his life and his dreams.

His eyes widened as he began to share about his life and what he thought was most important. He went on to tell me he felt like something big was going to happen to him, something amazing. His name was Matthew and his fiery enthusiasm was remarkable! His face was bright, his shoulders rocked back and forth gently, and his arms were in motion as he spoke about how he wants to be a better person every day. In contrast to this upper body animation, I noticed that his feet were firmly grounded to the floor. He paused briefly, taking in a deep breath. I asked what his favorite dream was. Without hesitation, he said, "I want to create a micro home in Montana that's completely sustainable and potentially off the grid!" and he sighed. He commented how awesome it would be if thousands of people did the same kind of thing.

I was inspired by his lust for life at such a young age and the wisdom and self-knowledge he possessed, and I told him so. I offered the old adage spoken so eloquently by Mahatma Gandhi, "You must be the change you want to see in the world." He was guiding his life in that very direction. We talked about how, if he keeps his eye on his goal and his heart leading the way, he would surely see all his dreams come to fruition. We might have continued our surprise encounter had he not heard his name being broadcast across the airwaves in the store, calling him to assist another customer in electronics. How fortunate I felt to have been in his company and shared a glimpse of his vision. A good day! A good reason to feel good!

A Passionate Teacher

Grocery shopping had become an unexpected adventure of its own while traveling around the country full-time. No two stores seem to carry the same products and if by a stroke of luck, you found one that did carry something specific, the store layout was incredibly different. It felt like you were scrambling your way through a maze. You would be baffled as to where items were, where you came in and certainly confused as to how you would find your way out! Hazards of the lifestyle, I soon realized.

I stopped at a store called PUBLIX. I couldn't find a particular item that I was sure I had purchased at a PUBLIX in a different state. I asked a young man to help and he made every effort to locate what I wanted. Finally, he checked with the manager and their store stopped carrying it. I thanked him and proceeded to the check-out line with my other items. He was also the bagger at that register and he offered to carry my goodies to my van. Again, I thanked him. We got to talking on the way to the van that was parked a good distance from the regular sized vehicles.

His name was Dakota and he had done quite a bit of traveling early in life with family and friends. He always enjoyed the driving no matter where he went. He recently moved from Florida to Alabama to begin what he referred to as "his new life." He had been studying at the University of Florida with a major in secondary education. He planned to teach English and incorporate critical and creative thinking skills as part of his program. Dakota sounded determined and passionate about his future and that can only lead to success in the classroom. I told him a few stories from my teaching days which we both enjoyed. There's a camaraderie among educators regardless of the subject or grade level or even the time during which a teacher was on "active duty." I believe it's because of the shared desire to make a positive impact on young minds, preparing them to be the leaders of the future. For me, even on the toughest day, there was still a sense that what I was doing was worthwhile. It was delightful to hear a young man with a vision for being a great teacher. We can't have too many dedicated teachers preparing our children to become quality citizens. I believe this is more important now than ever before.

Extraordinary Vision

Did you ever goof up and have it turn into something unexpectedly awesome? I did just that trying to make a campsite reservation. When I arrived at the campground and checked for my campsite packet, it wasn't there. Off to the visitor's center I went. There, I met Cheryl, who scrutinized her reservation list and didn't see my name on it. She offered a solution that I couldn't refuse. She could place me in a "host" site set aside for couples who were willing to perform certain duties around the campground for a reduced fee for their stay. However, since I wasn't going to fulfill a host's responsibilities, I could only use the electric.

"DEAL!" I followed her to the site and saw it was a paved slab! It had rained heavily the night before and most of the unpaved sites were muddy and slippery. This site was also situated directly across from the showers which was always a prime location in my opinion. That was my first bit of good fortune for the day. While I waited for Cheryl to retrieve my paperwork from the main office, I had the pleasure of meeting a gentleman named Wayne.

I was moaning and groaning about the damp dreary weather, and he called me on my self-proclaimed "positive thinker" title by reminding me that it was only water, and I was camping after all. Touché! I had to laugh at myself. I thanked Wayne for the humbling reminder!

Wayne was a volunteer at the visitor's center and described his position as one of honor and intrigue. Listening to stories about travelers' adventures, why they chose to stop at Starved Rock State Park, Illinois, and what they were most interested in seeing while they were there gave him great pleasure. He was known around the place as "Smiley" because of the constant expression of joy on his face. Wayne was tickled with my traveling objective because he apparently had some good news he was thrilled to tell me about. "I'm all ears. Let's hear it." I pulled out my little notebook and pen and sat on a bench with him.

He described the amazing challenge that he was going to undertake in a few weeks. Wayne had been preparing for a cross-country bicycle trip from Oregon to Virginia. Originally, he planned to go earlier in the year but a slight detour caused by carpal tunnel surgery altered his start date. He was currently awaiting his doctor's medical release while volunteering at the visitor's center. Once given the go-ahead, he would be flying to his launch site in Oregon where he'd embark on his "bucket list" adventure. He was an attractive man and in top physical condition. He would be carrying approximately forty-two pounds of gear on the bike, grub for two days at a time, water, and a tent with necessary accoutrements for any type of weather. The one thing he didn't plan to take with him was an itinerary! He was just going to go! I loved it! Then he nonchalantly told me something that nearly knocked me off my feet. "You know, there's no time like the present to follow your dream, so I'm going for it and intend to reach my destination before my seventy-second birthday, two months from now, because I have other plans for another adventure."

What an inspiration he was! I offered him a high-five and the very best of luck and I thanked him again for the reality check about my earlier moaning. What a great man with a big dream! Now, that man knows what makes him feel great - goals, adventure, taking care of himself, service, people and to be ALIVE!

Uncanny Perseverance

As I arrived at Brightwood Inn B&B in Oglesby, Illinois, I was greeted by a lovely woman named Sharon who checked me in and escorted me to my room. I love B&Bs. They were perfect changes of pace scattered throughout my three-year journey in my sweet little 19-foot bare-bones van. A thick mattress, a full tub, Egyptian cotton sheets, a fireplace, and a homemade breakfast that I didn't have to clean up from. Ah, yes!

On our way down the hall, I noticed two women from the cleaning staff sweeping up red rose petals and giggling amongst themselves. "The honeymoon suite?" I asked.

"A honeymoon like no other," Sharon replied with a smile and a giggle. I was officially curious.

Sharon asked if I wanted to hear about a rather unique couple and their love story. That was like asking me if I wanted a nutty coconut ice cream cone on a hot summer day! "Of course, I do!" Sharon proceeded to tell me about a couple who had been living together for twenty-five years. They loved each other very much. The gentleman asked his special roommate to marry him every single Valentine's Day for those twenty-five years. Every time, she refused his proposal without explanation, just "NO." His love for her, patience, and relentless proposals were impressive. Apparently, not deterred by her rejections to his heartfelt requests, he asked her again this past Valentine's Day. This time, for whatever reason, she said "YES!" The gentleman and both of their families were ecstatic. Family members came out of the woodwork to assist in making sure their wedding would be one for the books, a truly memorable event. They went all out. Bachelor and bachelorette parties were planned for the happy couple. A church wedding with live music, spectacular flower arrangements of plump pink roses and perky white daisies fastened to the end of each pew, bridesmaids and groomsmen in gowns and tuxes, and, last but not least, a flower girl and ring bearer.

Now that might not sound all that unusual even with the twenty-five rejected proposals, but the beauty of this story is that the flower "woman" and ring bearer were in their mid-fifties and the bride was ninety-two years old and her groom was ninety-five! I got so tickled. They stayed in the honeymoon suite over the weekend with champagne, strawberries, and fresh rose petals on their wedding night bed with a special accommodation of a first-floor room. The kitchen staff was very attentive in preparing their meals with the exact specifications honoring their dietary needs.

How awesome was that? According to the newlyweds, who clearly felt no allegiance to any type of social norms, there is certainly no age limit on tying the knot! I thought on the way to my room, *Good for those guys! Love knows no bounds. How old is too old to get hitched anyway? Who's to say that when the love bug bites beyond a certain age that getting married is a moot point? Congratulations, love birds!*

Reflections

Dreams are such blessings. Even at their infant stages, simply engaging the imagination can bring a huge smile to your face. Visions are free and unlimited. They allow us to revel in endless possibilities. Our creativity explodes like firecrackers on the Fourth of July. Dreams are one of the quickest avenues to feeling good. Since they haven't officially occurred yet, you can morph them into anything you desire. What a gift our imagination is. Use yours often and have fun. Enough concentrated focus on how wonderful you'll feel when your dream comes to fruition can only support its arrival into your experience. So, dream on, dream big, and feel the good feelings now!

In the previous stories, the first and last were visions that had already manifested. The three stories in between were still in various stages of "still to come." Yet each person or persons involved could feel the happiness the dream elicited, regardless of the stage of development it was in. They knew something very important. Feeling good, especially before your dream is realized, increases the chances of it becoming a reality many times over! After all, as Dan Millman says in his book, *Way of the Peaceful Warrior*, "The journey is what brings us happiness not the destination." Both are worth celebrating!

"Without leaps of imagination or dreaming, we lose the excitement of possibilities."

— GLORIA STEINEM

Chapter 8 - Surprise

Birthday Celebration at 35,000 Feet

I love birthdays, especially mine! My 2015 birthday was more memorable than most.

First, I turned sixty! Go, me!

Second, for my gift, my three sneaky children and sister conspired to organize a professional family portrait shoot at the studio in our local mall. Everyone showed up, too, and on time…mostly! What a blast! Waiting for over an hour didn't feel problematic because whenever we all got together, regardless of circumstances, our accumulated senses of humor reigned supreme…not in a loud way, but in a totally fun, silly, feed off one another kind of way. We were the life of the party in that waiting area. It was almost closing time before the photographers finally got to us. My grandsons were starting to fade fast but held up beautifully once we got into the actual room behind the curtain. They were now entertaining themselves with the props. More than 150 clicks and countless outbursts of laughter later, our photo shoot was complete and we all left with our pictures on a disk.

Third, as my gift to myself, I planned a twelve-day stay in San Diego, California, which was time and money well spent! I have chosen not to include the details of my experiences there because there were enough to fill another book. Instead, I'll share the craziest thing that happened on the flight across the country from Maryland to California. My best friend from high school, Sharon, went along. She planned to stay the first eight days and we managed to book the same flight out. We got situated on the plane quickly and easefully. After the usual drill, our section was entertained by the most incredible young man. He shared amusing flight stories, offered bits of wisdom, and made us all laugh. At the conclusion of his performance, Sharon told him I had recently had a significant birthday. Yes, she told him I turned sixty! He congratulated me and shook my hand. Seemed harmless and appropriate, right? Well, the birthday recognition didn't end there.

I had settled in nicely and was reading a book when the pilot announced we had reached 35,000 feet. Moments later, our attendant announced loud and clear that someone on the plane had recently had a very special birthday and was headed to San Diego to celebrate. Heads were turning so he asked me to raise my hand. With a face redder than a ripe tomato, I honored the request and the entire flight applauded and turned to look at me! I was feeling elated and mortified simultaneously and Sharon was totally thrilled with the entire scene!

About an hour later, our attendant came on again and this time he announced that the flight crew made me a birthday crown and would be presenting it to me as soon as I stood up. I was blushing like a new bride. As I stood up, two other attendants leaned over Sharon to put the crown on my head and as invited by the speaker, the flight sang Happy Birthday to me. It was pretty awesome, I must admit. I thanked everyone, even Sharon. I sat down to have the snack they brought to my tray…Teddy Grahams and a miniature of Malibu Coconut Rum. Somebody snitched! Sharon!

I must have dozed off because the next announcement from the pilot was that we were beginning our descent into San Diego. I was still a little out of it when I heard my name over the microphone from the front of the plane. The most unlikely, yet spectacular thing happened next. Our flight attendant asked me to come forward. I thought I was dreaming, except for the fact that Sharon was nudging me to stand up and move up the aisle.

"Here she is, the birthday girl. Judi, I mentioned to the crew and passengers while you were asleep, that it might be a fun idea to send Sharon and you to a great restaurant in town so you could celebrate in style. I passed around a brown lunch bag for birthday donations and it came back with almost $100.00 in it."

At this point, I was in tears. Passengers were clapping and smiling. He handed me the mic and for once in my life, I was speechless. I muttered a few silly words to express my gratitude to everyone, but that was all I had at that moment. In my heart, I wanted to say so much more. I wanted to tell them how honored and blessed I felt to receive such a lovely gift from people I didn't even know, but the words didn't flow. On the way back to my seat, nearly each person I passed shared their best wishes, beautiful smiles and a few high-fives. What a birthday...a perfect TRI-FECTA!

The Secret Behind the Grins and Giggles

Ten Thousand Villages is a fair-trade retailer in Vermont. I didn't even know what fair trade meant until I met Therese, the manager of this eclectic shop. She explained that, in a nutshell, it means that an agreement is made between the producer and the seller of an item. The seller agrees to pay fair wages and provide a healthy working environment to those producing goods in a developing country. That sounded like a place I would like to support. I thanked her and as I was browsing, I noticed a lot of hustling and bustling going on. People flittering about me with big broad smiles carrying loads of boxes and bags. I discovered why there was so much movement. It was new inventory day and displays were being redone and stock was being put away. I was still curious about the smiles.

At one point, an intoxicating aroma wafted out of the back room. I couldn't stand it any longer. I asked one of the employees. She giggled, trying not to choke with her mouth full. "It's cookie day!" She was gone in a flash.

Cookie day? Only moments later, Therese arrived on the "wide-grin" epidemic scene with a small tray of her homemade cookies and handed one more to each worker.

"Okay, what's up with the grins, the giggles and the cookies?" Therese laughed out loud. The day we get new inventory from various countries around the world excites us all and so we make it cookie day. Some folks say my cookies are the best they've ever tasted. They're quite simple really. I use Vermont whole wheat, local apples, and…" she leaned in, "the oats come from Quebec. I don't tell many people that, so mum's the word here in the store, okay?"

"Hmm…under one condition." Therese stood tall and leaned back with a quizzical expression on her face. "You must allow me to have the pleasure of the smile-producing magic firsthand."

"You've got it," she said eagerly walking into the back room with her empty tray. Moments later, I saw her curling her index finger, motioning for me to come in the back. I nonchalantly strolled over to the curtain. She held it open for me and said politely, "Have a seat."

I sat at a small bistro table and Therese brought a dessert plate with three cookies and a cup of tea and placed them in front of me. "There you go. Tell me what you think."

After I savored the aroma of the warm soft cookie in my hand, I took a bite rendering me unable to speak until I had finally swallowed. My taste buds were in heaven. "Therese, these cookies are magnificent; they're perfect. Not too sweet, just the right texture. Do I detect m…?"

"Shush!" she interrupted. Perhaps she anticipated my words. "That's the final secret ingredient. Only my grandmother, rest her soul, and I know it!" She sat down with me, bringing her own plate and cup of tea, and we chatted like old friends for quite a while. Funny how an insignificant event like walking into a shop to look around can evolve into such a pleasant and memorable occasion. Of course, I was sworn to secrecy before I left.

Adopted by a Young Family

Laid back and lovin' it! Some days are just meant to be lazy and this was one of them. I woke up to pouring rain that was replaced by a gorgeous dry blue sky by 10:30 a.m. After a late breakfast, I rode my bike around the flat but gravelly grounds which created a symphony of crackling pebbles as they flew out from both sides of my tires. I read sporadically throughout the day from my cozy tree-to-tree hammock. In between reads, I had firewood delivered to my site, made a fire, and spent a while gazing at the dancing flames while meandering in my dreamworld. All of this I highly recommend.

After eating a late dinner, I walked down to the lake where I met a lovely family: Ann and Mark and their two adorable girls, Emma, who was seven, and Leah, nine. We chatted a few minutes about camping and how beautiful a day it had been. They had an RV that stayed parked there at Dune Lake Campground in Coloma, Michigan, and they come up almost every weekend from where they live, weather permitting. Ann was intrigued by my travel mission of discovering good news. She didn't require any coaxing to share hers. She decided to change careers and enter a relatively new field of study called gerontology. This type of program focused on a comprehensive look into the care of our senior population, including the social, cultural, psychological, cognitive, and biological aspects of aging. Ann loves that kind of work. She spent time with seniors in their own homes, in centers, and in medical facilities. Her graduation ceremony was held yesterday, May 16th, and today was Mark's birthday: two pieces of good news in one spot.

After a great night's sleep, I went to Ann and Mark's RV to drop off one of my travel cards and Mark offered to give me a ride into South Haven with him and Emma to show me around. Ann was going to take Leah to soccer. Nearly speechless with excitement and surprise, I managed to utter, "Yeah, that would be great!" It was settled then. We would meet at their RV at 1:00 p.m.

Mark was a superb tour guide, and Emma was his adorable "copilot." The entire area was filled with colors, people, aromas, and waterfowl as well as visually appealing architecture. The cloudless sky with its blue hues, joined right in to top off the beautiful surroundings. We navigated through a community right along Lake Michigan. It felt like being at the ocean without the salty air. The lake was huge with royal blue and teal water swirling and shimmering in the sunlight.

With each turn of our heads was another sight to behold. Terrific little shops offered items for people to wear, adorn their homes with, and give as memorabilia. We even saw a pet salon carrying everything from homemade organic treats in a variety of shapes, sizes, and flavors to fashionable pet outfits for all seasons! It almost made me wish I had a dog, but not quite. There was kite surfing, a red lighthouse at the far end of the pier, and sailboats gliding in and out of the "no wake zone." Proud fishermen raised their catch with outstretched arms for the sightseers to applaud their success, and we all did with enthusiasm and admiration. One of my favorite aspects of the walk along the lake was the super friendly dog owners. They were willing to stop and allow you to have a brief, yet memorable experience petting their pride and joy. On our way to grab some grub, I looked up and spotted a bald eagle-shaped kite whipping around in the breeze. I had never seen one like that before, and I adore bald eagles.

Lunch at a quaint little pub consisted of two seafood sliders on mini pretzel rolls and coleslaw. Afterwards, Mark and Emma made a mad dash to the local homemade ice cream parlor. Being their guest, I could hardly refuse their offer to buy me a cone of the flavor of my choice, could I? I thought not. How ungracious would that have been?! Besides, I LOVE ice cream, so it wasn't just a gesture of politeness for me to indulge!

The last stop on our afternoon excursion was to buy smoked salmon, which I had never had. Mark raved about it and coaxed me into trying at least a sample. To my surprise, it was pretty darn tasty. I decided to purchase a piece big enough for dinner. On our way back to the campground, Mark pointed out several walking and biking trails and shared directions to a lovely uncrowded beach on the lake very close by that I might consider while in town.

To top off an already fabulous day, Ann and Leah were back from soccer and Leah was high scorer for her game! We all decided to celebrate by making s'mores at their campsite after dinner! Ice cream and s'mores in the same day. I was livin' the life!

Memorial Day Outing

Another fun-filled day! I had breakfast with Ann and Mark, where I met their friend, Sandy. She had the Down Under accent which was enchanting. I could have listened to her speak all day. Sandy dragged out the big map and the campground directory displaying hot spots to visit in the Vermont-New Hampshire region (my next destination). She and her husband, Doug, traveled extensively and knew all the insiders' scoop.

I spent the early part of the afternoon in my favorite hot spot, my hammock. As I stretched out, it occurred to me that at each stop along my journey I had met new campers and was steadily realizing what a pleasure it was to feel how much camaraderie can be found amongst strangers. This subculture of RVers seemed to always be in a good mood. They exhibited a laid-back temperament in their minute-to-minute and day-to-day activities and were always willing to offer help or invite others to join them for a shared activity. I had only been on the road a month and was getting accustomed to that way of life! Then I began to reminisce about my experience with Ann and Mark and the girls. When I booked an extended stay somewhere and had time to become friends with a family, it was quite a special experience. It was amazing how easy it was to just drop right in and join them and I loved it!

We had all decided to get together for a Memorial Day pot-luck cookout around 4:00 p.m. My old stand-by, deviled eggs, was my contribution to the much-anticipated feast. I made them for most potlucks, but that time I added an ingredient to give them a little twist, sweet potatoes. All twenty-four eggs were devoured before Doug finished grilling his mouthwatering BBQ chicken. Sandy and Doug had two daughters close in age to Emma and Leah, and the first thing they grabbed at mealtime was corn on the cob. With glistening hot melted butter smeared across their faces from ear to ear and nose to chin, and with no sound other than slurps, we adults couldn't help but laugh at them.

After dinner, Ann and Mark invited me to accompany them to the farm of friends who raised goats and chickens to get some of their delicious eggs. Madeline and Roland welcomed us and gave us a tour of the farm. We got to the area where the pygmy goats were gathered. To my delight, Roland came around the corner with a three-day-old pygmy wrapped in a blanket for me to hold! A second baby had been born a few days earlier as well. Despite my reluctance to put "my" baby down, I did at the suggestion of Madeline. She wanted me to see what happens when baby goats are left to their own devices on the ground. Mork, the one I held, began to prance, and dance, and hop, and jump with joy beyond description. I gasped happily! Then Mindy, the second newborn, unrelated to Mork, was brought onto the scene and there was an immediate party going on. Madeline played some music and the show escalated. I had never seen anything quite as adorable as these baby pygmy goats frolicking with each other. That was a memory that I can still feel to this day, six years later.

Having returned from gathering the eggs, Mark set up a karaoke machine for the four girls to entertain us with. That they did, adorned in boas, hats, and heels many sizes too big! They were perfect examples of stars in the making!

I had such a delicious day, filled with surprises and joyful moments with my new friends. In fact, every day I spent with them was wonderful!

Miracles at Trinity Heights

I spent the night at Walmart! Yep, I sure did! I needed to stop somewhere because of misjudging my travel time to the next campground, so I called to let them know I would be arriving a day later. The woman who ran registration asked where I was. When I told her that I was at a Walmart picking up a few groceries, she excitedly told me to check with the manager to see if I could stay there for the night. My ears could hardly believe what she suggested, but I did what she said and, sure enough, there was a certain area on their lot where travelers could park overnight. The manager was so accommodating. She went out to the lot with me and pointed to make sure I knew exactly where she was talking about. I thanked her and after my food purchase was completed, I drove around the side and, to my amazement, discovered eight RVs of all sizes parked there! The spot I chose was in between two very tall stacks of bagged mulch. Van-Go looked like a toy vehicle, but I didn't mind because there was plenty of light and it had a cozy feel to it.

The following morning, heading out toward Sioux City, Iowa, I saw an incredible sight. It was well off the road but still visible. Enormous metal replicas of Mary and Jesus were situated on grounds that were meticulously manicured. I wondered what this place was. I took the ramp off the highway allowing me to read the sign, "Trinity Heights." I drove through the gates and parked near the gift shop and information center where I discovered that this sacred place, though based on Catholic theology, offered a venue for prayer, solitude, and beauty to visitors of all denominations. My curious nature led me to explore the grounds which included lovely "silent" walking trails and benches for seated contemplation. Flowers, such as I had never seen before, stood erect, caressing the paths with a sense of pride in their own beauty. The statues I caught a glimpse of from the road were thirty and thirty-three feet tall respectively and created by a world-famous sculptor named Dale Lamphere. The figure of Mary moved me deeply in an unexpected way. As I stood and gazed up at her warm compassionate eyes and welcoming smile, tears rolled down my cheeks. The love surrounding me felt like a hug. My heart was racing, yet tranquil. I walked over to a bench and sat quietly for quite a while, feeling grateful for having spotted this treasure.

After a bit, I strolled over to the St. Joseph Center that was home to a life-sized wooden carving of the Last Supper. Jerry Traufler, an award-winning wood carver devoted seven years of his life to crafting this remarkable work of art. He used local models to assist him in designing the figures with human emotion portrayed in their faces. A greeter asked if I had any questions and, when I told him I didn't, he asked if I would like to hear about one of the multitudes of miraculous events that have taken place there. "Of course," I replied eagerly. First, he told me there were twelve small condominiums on the expansive property. About seven years prior, a man with terminal pancreatic cancer decided to move himself and his wife into one of the condos. His plan was to see that his wife wouldn't be totally alone when he passed. He wanted her to have caring people around her, have access to the peaceful gardens, and maybe even have the opportunity to do some volunteering.

Once they moved in, they noticed a statue of St. Peregrine in their yard, but didn't give it a second thought, considering where they were. For many months following their move, their visits to the oncology department continued to baffle the doctors. The man began to get a clean bill of health. The cancer had literally disappeared. The man continued to do very well and, on the day I was there, he was still healthy and enjoying time spent with his wife, their children, and grandkids.

I thanked the greeter for sharing such a beautiful story but I was unclear about the miraculous turn of events regarding the gentleman's health. He smiled and said, "It just so happens that St. Peregrine is the patron saint of cancer patients." I was stunned at the revelation. More than that, I was comforted to know that a compassionate, unselfish thought by a dying man became the renewal of his life.

Reflections

For our purposes, let's be clear that *welcomed* surprises are the topic at hand. I suppose unwelcomed ones might be referred to as shocks. A welcomed surprise is an unanticipated occurrence that pleases you, elicits feelings of joy, excitement, appreciation, and even love. It's hard to imagine a pleasant surprise when feeling good would not be automatic. Choose to be the recipient that recognizes the wonderment in surprises and basks in the fun of them, feeling grateful. Remember, chances are that whoever orchestrated your surprise will feel as good as you. In the case where another person is not involved, savor the surprise, and thank the universe!

Surprises come in many packages. Sometimes, you get tiny ones like spotting the first robin of spring outside your window or finding the missing sock the dryer ate last week. Other times, you're blessed with really big ones like, let's say, winning the lottery or receiving a proposal of marriage. Truth be told, big or small, these surprises really are not so different. Depending on your outlook, regardless of the size package your surprise comes in, you can choose to be excited or not. I recommend the former. Why? Because it feels good! I love to feel good, and I believe you do too.

> *"One of the most beneficial and valuable gifts we can give*
> *to ourselves in this life is allowing ourselves to be*
> *surprised! It is ok if life surprises you. It's a good thing!"*
> — C. JOYBELL C.

Chapter 9 - Synchronicity

Perfect Timing

Have you ever experienced an event in your life that was simply perfect, where each moment flowed into the next so effortlessly, it seemed surreal? One such moment for me was when I went to the waterfall at Galena Territory in Illinois.

The officer I met in Niobrara State Park told me about this place. He had grown up in Galena and suggested many wonderful places to see. Due to time constraints, I had to be selective. Of course, the place with a waterfall won over all the other options. I drove into a gorgeous golf community and noticed a man walking across the parking lot. I stopped to ask where the information center was. His name was José and he offered to drive there so I could follow him. A mile or so through the pristine lush green hills and windy roads, we arrived. I thanked the gentleman for his kind gesture.

I was greeted by a man behind a counter and no sooner did I tell him that I was looking for the waterfall, I heard a woman's voice from behind me offer to show me where it was if I met her at her car at the end of the parking lot. Wow! We arrived at the breathtaking waterfall whose steep flow was beaming with a blueish tint. My guide, MJ, and I began a conversation as spectacular as the view before us. She explained how the path to the falls changed dramatically after the flood in 2008. It started out narrow and rocky with broken branches scattered about. Now, after the reconstruction, it was carved out wide enough for at least six adults to pass. Upper and lower packed-dirt viewing platforms were added. I took pictures as the cascade's lower level crashed over boulders and splashed straight upward!

MJ recently retired but continued doing the same work as a volunteer. I asked what her job was. She had been instrumental in developing a veteran support network that serviced two counties. All those in need were welcomed without stringent eligibility requirements. Basically, that meant that all services including family support, peer counseling, and camaraderie were provided free and with confidentiality regardless of discharge status. The program started as a pilot that was government funded. When I talked with her in 2014, the funding from a grant was soon to expire. She and many others were working diligently to find a way to keep the services available to the veterans and their families. I thanked her for being such an integral part of an effort to prolong that worthy project designed to improve the quality of life for those who have risked theirs to save ours.

As of the writing of this book, October 2020, the programs offered by the Lake County Veterans and Family Services Foundation were thriving and expanding as a 100% donation-funded organization. More details can be found at https://www.lcvetsfoundation.org

MJ and I agreed that our meeting was a synchronistic event. She and I were mutually grateful for the precise timing of how we met. She was right there hearing my request, having no time constraints as a retiree, as I was searching for directions to get to the falls that she knew so well! When intentions are strong and there's no resistance, somehow all the pieces of the puzzle fall into place and a memorable scene is created! How wonderful it was to be a part of that puzzle.

Chance Meetings

My heart smiled as I learned more about the Center for Birds of Prey in South Carolina. What they were doing was nothing short of miraculous. Approximately 500 injured birds were brought to their facility each year. Typical injuries were from vehicle collisions, electric pole burns, and accidental shootings. The loving, dedicated, and highly qualified staff attended to these animals with the intention of sending them back into the wild. The animals' natural habitats were constructed as close to the real thing as possible during rehabilitation. The success rate was an impressive 65%. Birds who had healed well enough to live, but whose injuries were too severe to return to the wild, remained at the center and were cared for by staff with great compassion to ensure the animals' well-being.

After the tour, I met Jenny and Beth Ann during a presentation in the amphitheater. We chatted about the center and how we were touched by the story of the tiny barn owl that wouldn't come out of a tree after high winds. His wing was already damaged trying to get to safety and he needed care. Fortunately, he was spotted by a staff member, rescued from the high branch, and doctored right up. A few weeks later, he was good as new.

One thing led to another, as it often does, and I found out Jenny and Beth Ann were best friends who traveled whenever their work schedules allowed. Headed back to the parking lot, we arrived at my van. Beth Ann's eyes nearly popped out of her head with delight. She explained how much she loved Tinkerbell and was ecstatic to see one of her quotes on the side of my van. "Laughter is timeless. Imagination has no age. Dreams are forever." I took a picture of her and Jenny standing by the quote. They giggled like kids.

I invited them into my van for a "tour" and Beth Ann shared that she had been wondering what she will do when she retired the following year. She had considered traveling but with considerable trepidation, since she would be alone. She asked me a zillion questions about my own experience and was feeling inspired about the possibility of letting go of her fears and going for it!

In sharing about their recent travels, Jenny chimed in with a memorable experience they had. Jenny had a pet bulldog for many years, but it had passed away four years prior. She often considered getting another dog but couldn't bring herself to do it. The other day, Beth Ann and Jenny were walking along the beach at Isles of Palm where they were staying. Jenny mentioned that it was her deceased grandmother's birthday. She loved Jenny's dog almost as much as Jenny did. Jenny told her friend that she hadn't even seen a bulldog in a very long time and how cool it would be to spot one somewhere. Beth Ann agreed. They turned around to walk back to their hotel and right there on the beach was a woman walking her bulldog! Jenny could hardly believe what she was seeing. She asked to pet the dog. As she stooped down, that dog came directly over to her and licked her hand. His owner explained how rare that was and that Jenny must have a real affinity for bulldogs. Jenny looked up at Beth Ann and smiled. She thanked the woman, and they practically skipped back to their hotel with childlike giddiness!

I thanked them both for sharing their beautiful experiences, and I gave Beth Ann my number in case she had any more questions about traveling alone. I certainly remember how I wondered about everything from the logistics to my emotional response to traveling alone when I first decided to embark on this journey. Funny how I've met so many people I share a common thread with. I'm impressed by it more and more with each encounter.

First Meeting, or Not

After my son's wedding weekend, I drove a few miles further south to Bethany Beach, Delaware for my favorite beachy food (fries cooked in peanut oil with vinegar sprinkled on top) and my ocean fix before I continued my journey. I drove to the boardwalk area and parked. It was an unusually warm day for October, so I took a long walk on the beach. The pale blue sky was amazing. There was a softness about it, speckled with rows of small billowy clouds. I saw end-of-season sales everywhere, which called to me. I stopped at one shop and picked up a new sweatshirt on my way back to the van.

As I approached the van, I noticed a woman walking up to it. We introduced ourselves. Her name was Suzanne. She said she felt drawn to Van-Go, especially because of the uplifting quotes plastered over its exterior. She was hoping to meet the owner, then I happened by. Suzanne shared that she had purchased a similar style van awhile back, thinking she wanted to travel. Shortly thereafter, she realized the only place she wanted to go was the beach. Deciding to sell her van, she bought a small condo two blocks from the neighboring beach in Ocean City, Maryland. Our "chance" meeting seemed more like a reunion. It was like we knew each other prior to meeting that day. We talked for more than an hour about our adventures, life, similar rough times, and what traveling was like in Van-Go. Suzanne was beaming with bright beautiful energy from head to toe! Her smile was contagious, and her movements were soft and fluid when she spoke of the things she loved: her daughters and the ocean mostly. As we continued to share our passions, we realized we both adored watching the sunrise. We decided in that moment that we would be "sol" sisters and should keep in touch. We exchanged contact information, hugged, and went on our ways.

Within an hour, we had texted each other expressing our gratitude for having shared those unexpected yet memorable moments in time together. As of the writing of this book, October 2020, we are still in touch and closer than ever. Every time we met when I came into the area during my travels, we would walk the beach and blow bubbles at dogs and toddlers or just in the air. Five years later, when we walk on the beach, the bubbles still soar.

They say people can come into your life for a moment, a day, or sometimes for a lifetime. Our friendship is destined to be a lifetime kind of connection. You never know what blessings will show up when you least expect them. I know Suzanne and I are both grateful for this one!

During one of my many conversations with Suzanne, I mentioned that I was thinking about adding to my book the auspicious story of how we first met. She was so excited about this prospect that she exclaimed that she wanted to write her version of the story as well. Here's what my dear friend wrote about our first encounter.

Meeting Judi

"Early October 2015, the Universe dealt me a profoundly difficult hand. I had to make the choice to euthanize my beloved dog. I desperately wanted to save her, as she had saved my life when I adopted her three years earlier. On a lonely Friday evening, she and I walked into the vet's office and I stayed with her as her big white head fell into my cold hands. My heart broke that evening, and to this day, over five years later, tears still find my soul.

Two weeks later, on a beautiful early Autumn day, my daughter and I were visiting Bethany Beach, Delaware. After a sunny beach saunter and shopping trip, we were walking back to my car and I noticed a white van with cute quotes and little artsy designs all over the exterior. I looked at the custom art and read every quote. I didn't peer into the windows although my curiosity was bursting with intrigue. I wondered who could own this amazing vehicle. And just like that, the universe sent the owner. She walked up and we started chatting. I can't recall the immediate greetings exchanged, but what I do recall is the sincere connection I felt with this woman. Her name was Judi.

She was filled with enthusiasm for living, and equally happy to share her journey and wisdom. We visited and chatted for over an hour! Judi shared her 'Van-Go' intention with me – to gather good news and help facilitate good feelings throughout her cross-country travels. She was on an amazing journey and I felt privileged to have met such an inspiring person. I was thrilled and honored when she invited me inside her van for a 'Van-Go' tour. As Judi showed me her little artifacts and sentimental mementos, the grief over losing my beloved dog subsided. What a blessing! Who knew sharing time with my newfound friend and 'Sol Sister' (we shared a love for the sun), would go on record as becoming a highlight of my year? We exchanged contact information, said our good-byes, and parted ways. Today is November 23, 2020 and we're still Sol Sisters and share an amazing friendship. I'm forever grateful for that autumn day in Bethany Beach where I met Judi. Knowing her and watching her continue to find, inspire, and share goodness with others has been a wonderful journey in my own life. So, keep on sharing that good news with this world, my dear Sol Sister, Judi!"

How Did They Know?

At a potluck at one of the campgrounds, I walked out of the community center to find a spot to sit. Space was at a premium, so I sat where a couple, Cindy and Gary, were already seated. They welcomed me graciously. We discussed how delicious the food was and then shared a bit about ourselves. The couple was from Missouri, had been married for forty-five years, and, as Cindy put it, "We actually still like each other." That got an applause from me.

Then they shared a serendipitous story with me. A few years ago, they were considering going on the road full time. In the meantime, their grandson moved in with them for two years to save money for college. Gary commented, "Believe it or not, they were wonderful years for all of us. It was a joy to have a young person around. I think we learned a lot from each other."

After their grandson left for school, they got to thinking about their dream again. Their ideas were still in the infant stages. They hadn't really taken any steps toward making it happen. A week or so later, in the afternoon, Cindy heard a knock on their door. Outside was a real estate agent and a couple who inquired about buying their house. I could only imagine the shock on Cindy's face, considering their house wasn't even on the market!

"I was spellbound. I didn't know what to say. Gary wasn't home, so I gave them a price that I knew was way too high so they would leave. The couple whispered to their realtor for just a matter of seconds and came back wanting to make an offer. I froze. The realtor handed me her card and said she would be in touch in a day or so. I closed the door and sat down on the nearest seat in utter disbelief."

Her husband came home shortly thereafter and she explained what happened. Gary laughed and said how crazy it was and dismissed the entire situation. Two days later, there was no denying what had happened. The realtor did call and the couple was willing to pay the "asking" price in cash! Gary and Cindy talked it over and decided to go for it. "It was like someone

145

heard our thoughts, recognized our hesitation, knew it was time, and made it happen with an offer we couldn't say no to. It was like a miracle," Cindy told me. I was stunned. Actually, I was ecstatic. I love it when stuff like that happens.

With the buyers paying cash, a settlement date was agreed upon quickly. The couple was anxious to move in and requested that Cindy and Gary be out of their home in two weeks. Cindy said, "We were so excited after settlement, we made arrangements to comply with the new owners' wishes."

Gary explained how it went down. "We went that very next day RV shopping and found the perfect one for our needs. We got a fifth wheeler since we already owned a heavy-duty pickup truck. We had a couple of friends help us with clearing out forty-five years of accumulated possessions. Most things we just gave away, and our personal belongings required to live on the road went directly into our new home. I think we were in a state of shock throughout the whole process. It still feels kind of surreal."

When I talked with them, they had been on the road for three weeks and were loving every minute of it. I wished them the best and thanked them for sharing such an inspiring story. It makes you wonder.

Everything I Didn't Know I Needed

Wow! Stone Mountain, Georgia, was one campground where I didn't mind arriving in the dark. In fact, in this case, it was fabulous! Stone Mountain State Park was lit up for Christmas big time. It was just gorgeous! I certainly didn't expect that.

The next morning, when I opened the curtains at the back of Van-Go, I saw water! I was parked alongside the far end of a clear sparkling lake. Oh, yeah! Suddenly, I was extra grateful I had reserved two nights there instead of one like originally planned. I loved camping near water and had no idea there was a lake there. I must be smarter than the average bear! It was chilly but clear, and I spent some time at the wider section of the lake. The sunlight dancing on the water was mesmerizing. Boy, I could have hung out there a L-O-N-G time. Bedtime came early, though, to prep for a five-hour excursion in the morning.

I left pretty early to get a jump on the day, and by 9:00 a.m., I was starved. I had not been to the grocery store yet for my two-week stash, so Van-Go's cupboards were bare. I kept pushing my breakfast stop because there were no restaurant names I recognized on the highway signs. Then I saw IHOP. I knew *that* one! Well, I got off the exit and every establishment the signs had listed were there except IHOP. I rode up and down that street three times and nope, no IHOP. So, on the road I went another twenty miles only to see another IHOP sign. I was so hungry that I was more than happy to try again. Lo and behold immediately off the exit sat the IHOP! The only thing more delectable than my eggs, pancakes, and turkey bacon was Alicia, my amazing server. Aside from being pleasant, accommodating, and on the ball, she proved to be a light and joyful spirit! Our conversation started with me complaining about the unseasonably cold weather (frost warnings in Georgia, really?). Alicia, with a childlike smile on her face went on to say how much she adores the chilly air and the changing of leaves because it puts everyone in the spirit of Christmas. I had no comeback for that except for an inner feeling of gratitude to her for putting things in perspective for me.

We talked about the benefits of living with a positive mindset. She told me about the inspiring quotes she gets in her inbox every day from www.positivelypositive.com and how she looks forward to reading them each morning. Now, try to tell me that it was a fluke that the other IHOP couldn't be found. She gifted me with a reality check I didn't even know I needed.

I thanked Alicia for being there waiting for me because I needed a dose of her!

A Woman's Fortuitous Series of Events

Did you ever think you were going someplace for a specific reason only to discover that you really ended up there for an entirely different reason? I was pretty sure that's what happened to me when I planned my visit to Falling Waters State Park in Chipley, Florida. My intention was to experience peace and quiet and to sit and marvel over Florida's tallest waterfall at seventy-three feet. The pictures online I had seen during my research were gorgeous. In fact, I was so excited that I stopped there before I checked in at my campsite. As it turned out, it was more of a water-trickle instead of a waterfall because of the lack of rainfall that season! I stood and imagined the sounds of a cascading deluge and the mist on my face. Nice try on my part, but to no avail.

As disappointed as a child on Christmas morning who didn't get the one thing she wanted most, I arrived at the campground and parked on my site. I was thrilled to see two perfect trees for attaching my hammock. After I settled in from hooking up all the necessary apparatus, I read the park information guide only to see the words: "NO USE OF TREES FOR HANGING HAMMOCKS." It would cause major problems for the trees and there were specific sites that had large sturdy poles from which a camper could attach their hammock. My site was not one of them. *Okay, no big deal.* I hopped on my bicycle to get firewood from the ranger station, but they had just sold their last bundle. I didn't know whether to cry, scream, or just go to sleep. To add to the already sinking feeling in my gut, around 5:00 p.m., the neighboring site was having some sort of reunion, which included three adorable but noisy little ones that had very loud fun until about 10:00 p.m.

No waterfall, no hammock, no firewood, no quiet! I was striking out. The day wasn't a total loss because between the early disappointments and the crazy party, I did hike through some beautiful foliage on a path that led to a peaceful lake and I was able to capture a few breathtaking pictures of trees, bushes and the sky reflected on the lake's surface. Still, I was feeling like I didn't get anything I came for.

The following morning, an unexpected event occurred that shifted my entire perspective regarding the real purpose of this stop. Kim, a volunteer at the ranger station, came by my site and asked if she could talk to me a few minutes. First, she expressed how tickled she was about the quotes on Van-Go and walked around the van taking pictures of each one. Then, she thanked me with her beautiful smile for spreading joy everywhere I traveled. How sweet was that? Later that day, Kim came sprinting across the empty sites, taking a short-cut to mine, with her camera phone in hand waving at me. I came around the van to meet her.

"You have to see this, Judi. I can't imagine how this happened."

I looked closely at one of the pictures she had taken of my quotes the day before. On one of them there were streams of sunlight that showed up pink. It was spectacular. None of the other dozen photos had any sunlight at all. The quote behind the somewhat surreal photo was "Nothing is impossible...even the word says I'm possible." We sat and marveled over the mystery of it all.

After Kim left, I kept thinking about that pink-rayed picture Kim took, I decided to walk up to the ranger station to see if she could send me that picture on my cell phone. I found her making a unique garland for the station's light decorations. She asked me about the van in more detail and when I told her about my delight in hearing good news from people, she lit up like that garland and asked if she could share something. We sat on the bench outside the station to talk.

Kim had been looking for a part-time job for many months with no bites until her sister called her in October to tell her about this position. She called, was invited for an interview, went, and nailed it! She was offered the job on the spot. Kim grew up in natural surroundings and her gratitude and enthusiasm about having a job that allowed her to be amidst nature all day every day and get paid was contagious. I could feel myself wiggling in my seat like a kid waiting their turn to see Santa.

150

Kim proceeded to share several more events that had recently taken place in her life that she referred to as miracles. Having less money than she needed prior to obtaining this position, she sat one day about a week before the utility bill was due to come in the mail and imagined it in her mind being a particular amount much lower than the quarter before. When the bill arrived, it was for the exact amount she had envisioned. Then she was walking to the pharmacy to pick up a prescription and saw a wad of money scrunched up along the curb. She picked it up and counted $13.00. At the pharmacy register, the total rang up at $12.00. With the extra dollar, Kim bought a lottery scratch-off and won $2.00. She also needed a washer and dryer she couldn't really afford. She looked online for a good used pair and left a few messages. A woman returned her call within an hour, offering Kim just what she needed in fabulous condition for FREE!

Now, that was a woman living in the flow of life! Her lighthearted, childlike approach to her world with a little gratitude thrown in yielded her one serendipitous experience after another. I was, and still am, so grateful that she flowed into my life. Kim's vibrant spirit, I decided, was the real main attraction at this destination, not a waterfall, hammock, firewood, or quiet!

Reflections

The cool thing about events that seem to occur with no obvious effort on your part is just that: they are effortless. If you have ever experienced a synchronistic event, you may have recognized it as all the pieces of the puzzle amazingly fitting together with no reasonable explanation. It often feels like there's meaning beyond a simple coincidence. Being on the lookout for such events not only elicits good feelings but is also so much fun!

Oftentimes, you may not notice the synchronicity in a particular situation until it has passed. That's when the ah-ha's show up, also a lot of fun.

Mathematical law suggests that coincidence is simply a series of random occurrences that are bound to show up now and again in your life. However, when those events happen and they feel important to us in some way or have an emotional or physical effect on us, then they become synchronistic.

In the stories related to this theme, there is really no explanation for the timing or circumstances of any of the events. Of course, you could attempt to rationalize the sequence of events but, most likely, unsuccessfully. If an idea came to you that synchronicities may have something to do with the way a person thinks or what a person believes, you might be onto something. I figure that as long as you feel good and appreciate it when an unexplained good fortune or happy thing occurs in your life, your work is done. Appreciate it, marvel over it, and allow the mystery to intrigue you!

"Synchronicity: A meaningful coincidence of two or more events where something other than the probability of chance is involved."

—CARL JUNG

"Sometimes life drops blessings in your lap without your lifting a finger. Serendipity, they call it."

—CHARLTON HESTON

Did you know...?

You have about 60,000 thoughts

every single day.

Make as many

as you can

happy ones!

We assign meaning to everything: relationships, events, feelings, actions, places, songs, thoughts and so on.

YOU decide what label or meaning you assign.

Choose one that feels good.

Section 3 – Turning Points

As you will read in the next chapters, several events occurred that had my head swirling with confusion which led, over time, to the need to answer haunting questions.

Were there going to be yet more major decisions? Would those decisions, once again, change my life considerably? The questions didn't seem to cease.

Should I, or rather, do I want to continue on the same path? If so, how much longer would I travel and to where? If not, what would I do? Would I move back to Albuquerque? What will my life be like if I don't? Where would I go? Could I afford to settle down again?

Eventually, and quite unexpectedly, I found myself in a position where I became quite clear about what to do. How that happened, when and where is divulged in the upcoming chapters. Was the revelation destiny? Serendipity? Or a request from somewhere deep inside of me? I'm still not exactly sure. The only aspect of the answer that I was certain about was that it felt right.

Chapter 1 – A Shock to the System

*"Instead of worrying about what you cannot control, shift
your energy to what you can create."*

– ROY T. BENNETT

Tres Rios Resort in Texas is a place I will always hold dear to my heart. It's the place where strangers became family in a split second. A phone call from my doctor threw me for a loop. What started as a routine check-up turned into a need for emergency surgery. I was told I had a kidney stone lodged in my ureter blocking the flow of urine from my kidney to my bladder. Portions of my right kidney wall were stretched thin from the accumulation of backed up urine. The doctor was astounded that I had not experienced any pain when it should have been excruciating. His guess was that this had been progressing for about two years. He cleared his schedule to fit my surgery in for noon the following day. Once the surgery was complete, he would insert a stent into my kidney to remain in place for seven days.

Suddenly, I had a million emotions running through me. My mind, body, and spirit were in a state of shock and fear. A woman who was typically quite brave and independent found herself frightened and feeling alone. That woman was *me*!

My first rational thought was that I needed someone I cared about to be close to me. A small monkey wrench in that idea was that anyone who fit that bill was two-thousand miles away. I opted to step out of my comfort zone and ask for an "over-the-top" favor. I called my son and asked if he could fly out for a couple of days. He didn't even flinch and was able to get off work and fly into Texas from Maryland. Though his flight would not arrive in time to be with me before I went into surgery, he would be there when I woke up. What an incredible blessing that was for me, a gift I'll always cherish. I sat and cried in appreciation for his selflessness and love.

The next thought I needed to entertain was the hospital policy stating that someone had to be at the hospital with me during the surgery. I felt even more alone. What was I going to do? It was my first day at this campground which left me not knowing a soul. I decided to just ask. I walked into Texas Hall where a group of six campers was playing Dominos. I introduced myself and explained my dilemma. Uncontrollable tears of surprise and gratitude rolled down my face as each person offered to take me and stay with me. A woman named Deanna was the chosen volunteer.

Then, there was the fact that I was scheduled to leave that campground on Friday morning, now only two days after my upcoming surgery. I sought out the gentleman in charge of "everything." He looked up my membership plan and told me it wouldn't be a problem. In addition, I had a free week stay in a luxury cabin with my plan. My son, Matthew, would be able to stay with me in a roomy, comfy cabin with heat, hot water, a stove, and a real bed and bathroom. Matthew could sleep on the sofa the two nights he was with me. In addition, I was able to remain in the cabin for the duration of my recuperation.

The following day, the surgery went well according to the surgeon. The blockage was cleared, the stone removed, and my kidney, though still stretched out, was in great condition. Deanna stayed until Matthew arrived. Seeing my son when I first opened my eyes was like seeing an angel at my bedside. All stress just melted away.

Once the doctor released me, that same day, Matthew and I went out to lunch. Back at the park, we stopped in Texas Hall to say thanks again to all my other "angels" and let them know I was good to go. A round of applause followed. Matthew and I kicked back and watched a movie, then we talked for hours! We hung out at the campground and enjoyed each other's company the next couple of days. My son returned to Maryland and I rested the next four days before seeing the doctor for my follow-up and release.

Judi Ronco

Ready to head to the doctor's the following morning, I got into my car and it wouldn't start! Thank goodness I planned to make a few stops beforehand and was leaving a couple hours early for my appointment. I immediately went to Deanna's RV and asked her husband Wayne to help. He was available and I was happy that he was willing and able to check things out. My battery wasn't happy, but it did take a charge. Wayne followed me to Walmart where I bought a new battery. All the service bays were full and my wait time would have been over two hours, rendering me late for my appointment. But when I explained how crucial it was for me to reach my destination on time, the manager bumped me up and had me out of there in twenty minutes! Whew!

I saw the surgeon and, even though he didn't feel it was necessary to do any additional testing after the surgery, he assured me that the stone was gone and I could look forward to moving ahead without the concerns of dealing with urinary tract infections. I was relieved to hear his parting words as I left the hospital office.

158

Chapter 2 – Sudden Change in Plans

"When life becomes difficult, allow yourself to feel the
pain in the moment. Go with it for as long as it lasts, then
watch it dissolve away. Pleasure and pain are merely
states-of-mind. Every situation is neutral."

— DARNELL LEVIN

Completely relieved but exhausted after my kidney stone surgery, I decided to make a stop in Albuquerque, New Mexico before I continued my adventure. For several weeks, I took it easy, recouping at my friend Jean's home. She took wonderful loving care of me as she does with all those in need who are blessed enough to cross her path. For several days, I was feeling stronger and more alive again when suddenly I came down with a fever. I went to the doctor and damned if I didn't have another urinary tract infection! The surgeon in Texas told me I'd be done with them now that the kidney stone was gone. I was furious and frustrated. After a round of antibiotics, I did feel better physically. However, I knew I needed to cancel all my plans to visit more of the country and create a route directly to Maryland where my family was and seek out a new urologist. All I did was drive, eat, and sleep for four days.

When I got to Maryland, I found a wonderful urologist. After an array of tests and examining the reports and pictures sent by the surgeon in Texas, it was discovered that the kidney stone had *not* been removed. It was only reduced in size enough to unblock the ureter where it was lodged allowing it to shoot upward and land smack dab in my right kidney. When I told the doctor that the surgeon hadn't done any tests after the surgery to confirm the removal of the stone, he was appalled. Nonetheless, there was nothing that could be done about that error. We could only move forward. The urologist scheduled me for a lithotripsy (shock wave therapy using ultrasound) to pulverize the stone into small enough fragments that could pass through me.

The procedure was completely successful and over the course of a week or so, the fragments were released. Many follow-up tests were taken to insure the

159

absence of the kidney stone. Both the doctor and I expected that I would be pain-free at that point; however, the pain in the lower right section of my abdomen, near my right hip, became increasingly worse. As it turned out, I was experiencing some arthritis in the joint connecting my hip to my thigh, and my doctor recommended physical therapy.

I was packed up and planning to leave with my grandson to travel across the country in just four days! I contacted a urologist and potential physical therapist in Albuquerque, set up an initial appointment, loaded up on Ibuprofen, and off we went as planned.

Chapter 3 – Joy of My Grandson's Presence Prevailed

*"Things turn out the best for people who make the best of
the way things turn out."*

– JOHN WOODEN

My daughter Nicole and I planned for my grandson, Cameron, to spend most of the summer with me before all the physical drama. I couldn't bear to disappoint him, so we made it work with the help of the doctor and his prescription for 800 mg of Ibuprofen twice daily until we arrived in Albuquerque nine days later. I designed a workbook for my grandson, including games to play on the road like Hangman and a state license plate search. We had a blast together!

We had adventures every day, it seemed. According to Cameron, crossing the Mississippi River, making new friends, playing pool, and visiting Dorothy's House and the Land of Oz in Liberal, Kansas, were definite highlights to stash in his memory bank. However, there were a couple highlights we both would prefer *not* to have experienced. One night, it was 92 degrees in the van with only a tiny area fan to cool us. Another bummer was discovering the famous Pancake House on Pancake Blvd, just down the road from Dorothy's house, was CLOSED when we arrived with our mouths watering. We survived!

All our campground stops were for one night only because we were anxious to get our summer started in Albuquerque. Nonetheless, we had a ton of fun at each place. We met other campers, made s'mores, got the best out of what nature had to offer, swam in really big pools, *and,* last but not least, stayed up late eating junk food and watching movies or playing games.

After nine days and about 1,900 miles, Cameron and I arrived in Albuquerque! We stayed our first night in a campground because my apartment I had lined up was completely naked. The next morning, friends gathered to help drive to several areas of New Mexico to gather what I had in storage in other friends' garages. It was sheer craziness. Thank goodness for vans, pick-up trucks, and strong backs.

Apartment #1 – Once all my items were at the apartment complex and my angel helpers and I started lugging everything up thirty-six steps to the third floor, the pain in my hip grew worse. By the second day, trying to be the fun active Grammy that Cameron knew had become nearly impossible. While painfully traversing thirty-six steps several times a day to and from the pool and playground, I realized a third-floor apartment wasn't going to work for me. To add to the discomfort of those first several nights, there was no air conditioning. I began physical therapy on day four and the therapist said I needed a first-floor apartment. Fortunately, we had only unpacked the kitchen and bathroom and had been sleeping on a recliner and an inflatable mattress.

Apartment #2 – Dreading the next morning having to ask the office staff if there was a first-floor apartment available, I didn't get much sleep. Despite my trepidation and fatigue, I limped in the front door of the office the following morning with a letter from the physical therapist and pleaded my case. The best they could do was have one ready for me in eight days. Cameron, being the sweetheart that he was, conceded to playing in the apartment with only one daily trip to the pool and living out of boxes until we were able to move.

A second team of "muscle" was gathered for the second move in less than two weeks. To this day, I'm eternally grateful for my angel team. It got a little crazy preparing to move again, but we seemed to make the best of it. The move itself went very well. The new apartment was just around the corner from the first one. We unpacked everything in only two days. Cameron and I celebrated life without boxes! The air conditioner worked great and, for two whole nights, Cam and I slept like babies. Then the "real" fun began. It seemed that the upstairs tenant was at the hospital those first two nights having her third child. Then they came home and wreaked havoc every single night with stomping, screaming, slamming, and so on. The office staff spoke to the mother several times to no avail! Ear plugs helped somewhat, but our hands were tied. We had to make the best of it.

My appointment with the orthopedic surgeon confirmed the arthritis in my right hip and low spine. The treatment plan consisted of physical therapy at the clinic, at home exercises, and the continued use of prescription strength Ibuprofen for a while. I was given the go ahead to explore with my grandson as long as I kept tabs on the pain and didn't overdo it. He assured me that I would make great strides in my therapy.

My grandson and I did have quite a few adventures over the month following the move, especially the many trips to the pool that was only a three-minute walk. We went to the Science Center one day then to Old Town Square for lunch. Our restaurant had a tree growing right smack in the middle of the room! Cameron had his first sopapilla with honey. The nectar was dripping down his chin reminding us of Winnie the Pooh! We laughed and laughed. Best dessert ever. YUM!

We also ventured to the Rattlesnake Museum. That was Cameron's idea! To my surprise, I actually found many of them to be beautiful. Cam held a couple of big snakes under the supervision of a museum aide. I touched one which was enough of a hands-on experience for me.

The fun continued almost daily with a Mariachi Band in the gazebo in Old Town, and a special movie night at the apartments, showing *The Sandlot.* Rain showers prior to the movie left an amazing double rainbow which Cameron had never seen. One entire day we spent at the Bio Park which included the Aquarium, the Zoo, and the Botanical Gardens. To give Grammy's hip a break, we spent several days on the patio working on a project refinishing a three-tier corner shelf. We sanded, painted, and decorated. It looked fabulous. We were so proud of ourselves.

At the Route 66 Summerfest, Cameron got on a crazy ride that rendered him immobile for about thirty minutes. My heart went out to him as he sat on the curb with his head bobbing between his legs saying, "I think I'll just sit here a few minutes, Grammy. It was horrible!" It was blazing hot. Eventually, we stepped into a cafe and got a cool fresh smoothie. It helped enough to get him back to the apartment.

Time flew and suddenly it was time for Cameron to go home. Nicole and Cam's Aunt Terri arrived early evening on a Monday after a twenty-eight-plus-hour drive across the country. To say that mom and son were happy to see each other would be a gigantic understatement! As soon as he laid eyes on her, he ran, jumped, and threw his legs around her waist and squeezed her like a roll of Charmin. After the excitement settled, we managed to sleep fairly well, considering the noise above us.

We all piled into Nicole's car early the following morning headed for the Grand Canyon. Our plan to see the sunset there was compromised by car issues, so we spent the night in a hotel and got back up at 3:30 a.m. to catch the sunrise. We all agreed it was worth it. We all had a marvelous time. Even though it was my third visit to this spectacular vista, my heart nearly skipped a beat at first glance. The sun over the canyon made the deep gorges and craggy walls glow like they were radioactive! Cameron climbed fearlessly up, over, and around as many rock clusters as he could manage, while us three adults watched with sweaty palms and gasps of breath. It turned out to be a perfect parting adventure, although it didn't make our good-byes any easier the following day. Watching Cameron and my daughter embark on their arduous two-day journey back to Maryland left me with mixed emotions.

My time with Cameron will always remain a precious gift, despite all the drama around my hip and the two moves! He's a teenager now, and he still remembers a good bit of our adventure. That makes my heart sing and tickles my funny bone!

Chapter 4 – Not My Final Move

*"Trust your hunches. They're usually based on facts that
are filed away just below the conscious level.*

– DR. JOYCE BROTHERS

Back to the new first floor apartment! I decided, maybe a month in, that I would view the woman's position of being alone with three kids under the age of five, one being a newborn, in a different light. I planned to muster up some compassion, and when I heard all the disruptive noises, to think of them as signs of new life and ignore them as much as possible. I also left the apartment at peak noise times on many days!

During the third month, I took walks around the complex looking for an apartment that I would *love* to be living in: one with all the features that I really wanted like a second-floor top unit, facing the front of the complex with a view of the mountain. I discovered three, one of them being my all-time favorite. So, one day, I decided to go to the office and just have them put those "preferred" units in my file for whenever. When the woman told me that my favorite one would be available in forty-five days, I got goosebumps! When she added that it had vaulted ceilings, well I knew right then and there that it was a gift. After much discussion with the manager, my transfer was approved. *I would be moving into my ideal apartment in just twenty-two days*, the Saturday after Thanksgiving! Could the timing have been any more perfect given the immense gratitude I was feeling? Once the amazement settled, I began to ask myself the following questions about my decision to *move again!*

Did I have to pack everything back up? YES.
Did I have to schedule movers and a truck again? YES.
Did I have to pay an apartment transfer fee? YES.
Would I need to pay transfer fees with the utility companies again? Probably.
Would I need to notify a bunch of people and places of my new apartment number? YES.
Is any of that a problem? NO! NO! NO!

Dear friends volunteered to help with the packing, and we made it a party!

In my new and third place, I had a delightful view of the mountain where I could see the sunrise. The wonderful light enabled me to have plants. Being on the top level, I was freed of the overhead noise. Walking up only one flight of stairs gave me just the right amount of exercise. The vaulted ceilings provided a more spacious feel. I was closer to the mailboxes, pool, and gym. My favorite apartment with an open view of the sky had become available just before the winter months when natural light is at a premium. What a blessing! I was thrilled! Finally, I would be settled in after more than three years on the road. YES! Back home! I could take a hot bath every night if I wanted to.

Memories of those four years I lived in New Mexico prior to my once-in-a-lifetime adventure living on the road were resurfacing. A particularly wonderful memory was the gathering of shamans for drum circles, workshops, journey sessions, and fire ceremonies. Spending time with like-minded friends, laughing, meditating, chanting, and doing energy work were experiences so precious that few words could sufficiently describe them. The best I can do is say that *it felt natural, it felt good.* I always came away from an event either lighter and more joyful than before or at least having more clarity around an issue. I participated in a very special overnight program in early spring 2018. My delight in seeing so many old friends expressed itself in hugs, smiles, tears, laughter, and more hugs! We spent much of the eighteen hours in silence contemplating the wonderment of our own divine nature and walking through the desert surrounding my friend Jean's property. I was feeling the beauty within me and around me. I was also experiencing some sort of turbulence deep inside that I knew might require some attention at some point.

Suddenly, during a lovely afternoon walk, I began feeling confused about my life. I was very hot and a little shaky, so I asked someone to get me a glass of cold water. When they handed it to me, I took a sip, then had an uncontrollable urge to pour it over my head. With that motion, I sat up quickly as my mind began to spin. A barrage of thoughts regarding my place of residence reared up and surprised the heck out of me. I thought I had figured it all out. Albuquerque would be my home like it was before my crisscross-country adventure. It seemed not. After several moments of a teary response, I received a clear message that I needed to move back East where I would "find love and more healing." You could have knocked me over with a feather.

I sat in that newfound awareness for a while. The mesmerizing sound of a violin and hypnotic flute music being played by the host filled my being with a sense of peace and I danced freely in and around the yard onto the desert floor. Thoughts floated through my head leaving me soothed, yet slightly unsettled. I recognized the feeling of absolutely needing to follow my intuition. It was the same knowing that I had when I first moved to New Mexico, and then again when I went on the road. I had learned to trust it even if I didn't quite understand it...yet! Still, a rush of fear, then anticipation, then relief coursed through my veins. My very soul felt like it was on fire. I made my way back to the house to get some nourishment to ground myself and I wondered, *What now?*

Did you know...?

There are 168 hours

in a week.

Can you commit to

choosing a minimum of

1 hour a day

to feel good?

At day's end, ask yourself, "How did I feel today?"

Be content with whatever your answer is and

choose to feel even better tomorrow!

Judi Ronco

Section 4 – Phasing into My New Life

As you can imagine, after my experience at the program, I realized I was going to be preparing to move yet again. The details were not a concern because, somehow, I knew it would all work out for me. Things always had; however, I wanted to do my part. I trusted that whatever I needed to do or whoever I needed to contact would be revealed to me when the time was appropriate. I would know where to move, when to move, and how to move.

What I found to be particularly interesting was the message that came with the clarity to move back East. "You will find love and more healing" kept echoing in my mind. I was certainly not seeking to enter into another romantic relationship, but I was up for increased well-being that might be coming my way. Can't have too much well-being, I figured. I was sure I would find out when the time was right. Answers have always come when I needed them. There was no reason to think otherwise this time.

As it turned out, I was not disappointed. An unforgettable moment a couple weeks later, during a dream that would change my life forever, I knew I would be moving somewhere very close to the Atlantic Ocean. Sobeit.

Chapter 1 – The Search for a Place to Live

"Each day comes with its own gifts. Untie the ribbons."

— RUTH ANN SCHABACKER

The town for me to seek housing in became clear while sitting for meditation one morning. Then the search was on for a year-round house rental. You wouldn't think that would be a challenging venture. As I researched, I discovered that most people who owned a home in Delaware near the beach rented only during the high-season from May to September or the off-season from October to April! Confident that that was where I needed and wanted to be, I kept plugging away. What made the search even more challenging was that I was doing it in late September from New Mexico because I wanted a house lined up for when I got there. I wasn't scheduled to move until mid-November when my apartment lease was up. One day, I was browsing online through the rentals in the Bethany Beach local paper and spotted one! I called the number immediately. The owner was kind and took all my information. She was planning to send me the full application. When I mentioned the time that I'd be moving to town, she hesitated. She and her husband were intending to have it rented out asap. Our conversation from there was one of near begging on my part and compassion overriding income on her part. An agreement was reached. Once my application was approved, I would send her the one-month security deposit and the full November rent. And so it was.

I was so grateful for having found exactly what I wanted. It was a townhouse less than three miles from the beach. It had two bedrooms and the bonus of a three-season sunroom off the back with lots of windows and lots of light. The price was perfect.

The week before moving day, I spent time in the Sandia Mountains, hiking and watching over Albuquerque and the desert from my favorite spot in the Elena Gallegos Picnic Area. The view was spectacular. The big bustling city, the vast quiet desert, and the strong majestic mountains, all from one seat! I was able to accomplish one more project before I left. Something I've always wanted to do was create an item that contained stained glass. With enormous assistance and most materials from my friend Cheryl, I created a serving tray with a stained glass insert. I learned so much. We had a terrific time throughout the entire project, and it turned out beautifully. I couldn't thank her enough. My friend, Dolly, painted a gorgeous landscape view of the area, including a few hot air balloons, and even framed it for me. My friend, Allen allowed me to take a one-of-a-kind hand-carved alabaster sculpture with me with a note to pay him when I had the money. My friend, Meghan would be dropping my keys to the office on the last day of my lease. Another friend, Cora, offered to pick up my daughter Rachel and her wife, Megan, from the airport the morning of the move. What a lifesaver she was. I had the girls flown in from Maryland to help with the three-vehicle drive across the country.

Chapter 2 – Moving Week Rollercoaster

"A misty morning does not signify a cloudy day."

— ANCIENT PROVERB

Everything was packed. Finally, it was November 11, 2018. It all suddenly seemed real that I was moving across the country *again*! The movers arrived on time. My special angels Christopher, Tiffany, Brian and Susan were there ready to make things happen. Jean and James stopped by to give me a parting gift, to share amazing hugs, and well-wishes.

Breakfast burritos were on hand for energy boosts. All was going quite smoothly until we realized that not everything was going to fit in the Budget truck. After much deliberation, a few phone calls, having Cheryl agree to drive fifty miles to pick up the sofa-bed, paying the movers extra money and giving them a few items, the truck door finally *closed*!

Rachel, Megan, and I went to grab some grub, so once we got on the road, we could cruise. We returned to the apartment parking lot, lined up all the vehicles for ease of hook-up and departure when I realized I didn't have the key to unlock the hitch on the back of Van-Go. I remembered seeing it in a baggie somewhere recently, ugh! For over an hour we made a ton of phone calls on a Sunday trying to find a locksmith. Shortly after we found *one* and he was on his way, I found the key! We called the guy immediately and apologetically canceled his service. He was not happy.

Megan and Rachel were in the Budget truck following me in Van-Go hauling my Ford Fiesta. We were on the road sailing smoothly for about thirty minutes. Then we ran into a freak snowstorm. The snow was pounding our windshields creating a nearly "no see" situation. My son Matthew, while in Maryland, put us on speaker while he was checking a map to find us a different route. We rerouted ourselves, driving a few hundred miles farther south than planned to bypass the weather. We crossed the Texas line with the snow still coming down strong. We had to stop and spend the night in a hotel. Way to start, already a day behind!

Long story short, it took us six days instead of the planned four, most of which were driven in either snow, rain, or fog! We had to stop every night to recoup! One amusing anecdote is that one of the hotels had a hot tub and we were pretty achy from tense driving conditions but had no swimsuits. Megan and I got very resourceful (desperate, actually) and got in with undies and long tank tops. Rachel sat enthralled with the unforgettable sight in front of her! Fortunately, no one else was in the pool area! Another instance of using our noggins to be resourceful was when we needed to spread jelly on bread and had no utensils and we used the end of a toothbrush handle! It worked perfectly.

We arrived at Rachel and Megan's house in Maryland on the sixth day. It was late afternoon, Friday, November 16th. Exhausted but ecstatic that we arrived safely and still talking to each other, we dismounted from our perches and hugged and hugged and laughed and cried. Waiting there was my son Matthew, my sister Tanya, and her wife Amy, ready to make the last leg to my house in Delaware. The girls had to work in the morning and needed showers and a good night sleep. I'll be forever grateful for their love, time, patience, laughter, and everything else it took to make that trip!

The move began with a multitude of temporary setbacks, but it all worked out in the end. It was rough going in the feel-good department for a while. Between keeping our sense of humor intact and expressing gratitude throughout the trip for staying safe, we managed to survive the craziness of the entire experience. Go, us!

On our way to Delaware, I drove the van with my Ford Fiesta in tow. Matthew took over the Budget truck, and my sister and Amy drove their car. We arrived about 8:00 p.m. The truck was empty about 11:30 p.m. or so! By midnight, my three amigos were on their way back to Maryland to hit the hay. It sure did take a "village" to get me to my new home! My heartfelt appreciation for

175

every single person who helped me from weeks before I left to moving day to the drive to unloading. I was truly blessed to have such a beautiful family and group of friends! The following few weeks, my time was split between creating a "Judi house" and walking on the beach. Both were like a dream come true and just in time for the holidays.

Chapter 3 – The Holidays with Family

"It's not what's under the tree that matters, it's who's around it."

– Charles M. Schulz

The Holidays with family and friends in Maryland after I got settled into my new home in Delaware was great. First, Nicole, Cameron, and I participated in the Turkey Trot very early Thanksgiving morning. Then there was the annual Thanksgiving breakfast at my sister's house. As I mentioned earlier in the book, she started that wonderful family tradition when I moved to New Mexico eight years ago. They always sent me pictures, but that year, I was there in person! It was such a warm and loving experience being able to hug for real. After filling our tummies with every breakfast food imaginable, the guys slipped into the family "fat and happy nap" which was also part of the tradition. We girls sat around the table chatting and catching up with each other.

December was a busy month. I had a couple friends come and stay with me for a few days. Dena and I played Scrabble and went dancing. Dressed in so many layers we could hardly bend over, Sabrina and I collected shells along the beach. My friend Alysia was in town from China visiting her family in Pennsylvania for the holidays. She drove south and I drove north a couple hours in horrendous weather to meet for dinner at the Cheesecake Factory. We had a fabulous visit eating amazing food and having great conversation. My grandsons Cameron and Jay had their first winter concert at middle school. Cameron played the French horn and Jay sang in the chorus. They were terrific! I braved the beach alone at least four times a week capturing sunrise shots. The seasonal highlight in beach towns was the annual Polar Plunge. Over two hundred people jumped into the ice-cold ocean. Unbelievable!

Christmas day, my oldest daughter, Rachel, hosted a pop-in potluck lunch party. I hugged friends I hadn't seen in years. Gifts were being tossed through the air or passed relay-style. We had no other options as the dozen or so kids had the floor covered with torn wrapping paper. Aside from being with family and friends, my second-best Christmas gift was the one I gave myself. Stuffing and dressing "Faith" from the Build-a-Bear store appeased my childlike spirit that year. Of course, I wanted no part of choosing a bear like most people do! Faith was a light-gray fluffy-tailed bunny with pink on the inside of her ears, feet, and nose. The salesgirl and I spent over an hour choosing the perfect wardrobe to accompany my new friend!

On New Year's Eve, I had a strong feeling that 2019 promised to be a fresh start for me. I could feel it from head to toe. My home was cozy, my heart was happy, my health was great, my kids were fairly close, and I was less than three miles from the ocean! I figured if I were going to live in a place that got really cold and snowy in the winter, it might as well be at the *beach*!

Just when I thought things couldn't get any better...

Chapter 4 – Magic on the Beach

"Sometimes, it's the smallest decisions that can change
your life forever."

— KERRI RUSSELL

It was an unseasonably warm day on February 5, 2019. The sun and sixty-five-degree temps brought sunbathers and sandcastle builders flocking to the beach. The new moon occurred the evening before which meant, for me, a hot early morning bubble bath. I greeted the sun that morning first. Then I returned for my ritual bath with bubbles, candles, and incense, creating the intention to be aware of any guidance for the upcoming month. I relaxed into letting go of any thoughts, fears, or behaviors that no longer served me. The me that evolved during my three years on the road beckoned for the awareness of the good in each day and feeling great about it!

After two months of typical winter temperatures, I, too, was drawn to the beach that afternoon. About 1:30 p.m., I grabbed a book and my beach chair and off I went to bask in the unexpected gift of warmth on a February day. My focus alternated between the words on the pages and the beach scene set against the ocean waves. At one point, I glanced at the shoreline and noticed a gentleman walking along dressed for a regular winter day donned in a jacket, scarf, hat, khaki pants and laced up boots. He didn't look at all like he knew the area or what the forecast was for the day. I didn't pay him much mind at first. I went back to reading. The next time I looked away, there he was, standing as still as the air and gazing into the vastness of the ocean. It seemed odd, but my attention returned once again to my book. It was at least thirty minutes later before I was compelled to break from my reading and to my surprise, there he still stood. Okay, by then, I admit I was a bit curious about this foreign figure. I sat watching him, wondering, making up scenarios about who he was, why he was there, and so on. I tried to continue reading, but when I noticed that I had read the same page three times over, I stopped.

I had been sitting for over an hour. A walk down the beach seemed in order. Contrary to my usual behavior, I decided to ignore him completely and walk behind him on my way. I decided that if he was still there when I turned to come back, I would walk in front of him, but not look at him, no eye contact. To this day, I don't know why or where such a plan came from. I walked about ten minutes with what his "story" might be on my mind the entire time and when I turned, I could barely see him in the distance. I began what turned out to be my fateful walk north along the shore while focusing on the ocean and small children playing in the sand.

Steps away from crossing his path, I heard a voice say, "Excuse me."

I looked up and inquired, "Me?"

He said yes and asked me to do him a favor.

My snappy reply was, "Well, it depends on what it is."

He smiled and asked my opinion about something regarding the ocean. We introduced ourselves. His name was Bob. He lived in Virginia and hadn't been to the ocean in quite a few years. That morning he woke up and decided that that day was the one and he got in his car and drove four hours to *my* beach! We talked for quite a while about our careers, our children, our previous marriages, and many other topics. We seemed to have a great deal in common. It felt easy to share my feelings about things with him. He was interesting and unpretentious. Though I was thoroughly enjoying our delightfully unexpected conversation, I had reserved a study room at the local library and had to leave. I handed Bob my card and told him if he was ever in town again, answering an urge to see the ocean, to call and I'd be happy to take a walk with him. Before I reached the library, three minutes away, Bob texted me saying how nice it was to meet me and how much he enjoyed our conversation. Fifteen minutes later, his text message was an inquiry about a possible lunch the following week. By the next morning, we had set up a visit for lunch on February 14th.

When I saw him standing on the ramp that led to the beach at high noon that day, I was so happy that he showed up, I couldn't stop smiling. He had turned and noticed me walking toward him and headed toward me. He gifted me with a beautiful wrist corsage. I put it on immediately and thanked him. We had lunch in downtown Bethany at the Ropewalk Restaurant just a few steps from the boardwalk. Bob and I spent the entire day together. It seemed that he was hopeful that we would get along well because he had reserved a hotel room in a neighboring town. That allowed him to return the following day to spend most of it with me before he headed back to Virginia.

After that first date on Valentine's Day, we spent time together nearly every day as we took turns visiting each other in our respective states of residence. Two months later, he sold his house of twenty-six years in Virginia and moved to Delaware. Two months after his move, I broke my lease and moved in with him. An interesting aside was that I found him the house he moved into that would later become our home.

One year to the day that we met, we got married, February 5, 2020. Our beautiful intimate wedding touched the hearts of everyone in the room. The love between us was palpable. Every month since we met, I made a list of things I was grateful for in our relationship totaling five hundred plus items. It has been nineteen months as of this writing.

I think back to the hot bath I took the morning of our first meeting, my intention to be aware of any guidance and the wisdom I learned during my Van-Go adventure. Choosing to notice at least one good thing each day, being open to surprises, feeling the connectedness among us all, and being sincerely grateful for every single breath, I am certain that mine and Bob's meeting was no coincidence, but a serendipitous event for sure! Recognizing things to be grateful for is a game changer. Make no mistake about it!

See for yourself.

Judi Ronco

Did you know...?

When you woke up today

you could choose to be

more than mediocre.

Set your sights on progress instead of perfection.

Any choice of a forward-moving nature will take you closer to surpassing ordinary.

Remember, it's the journey...so keep on keeping on with joy.

Section 5 – Awesome Extras

I chose not to refer to this final section as the Conclusion because it is intended to be more of a beginning. Section 5 – Awesome Extras is devoted to providing you with several BONUSES. It's absolutely an integral feature of the book's purpose as a whole. Please don't pass it by. It is quite an eclectic compilation of material. The selections consist of items designed to be challenging, thought-provoking, entertaining, enlightening, and beneficial in assisting you as you move toward a greater feel-good life!

But don't try too hard. Relax into your new feel-good perspective.

Remember, the point here is to feel good as often as possible. Trying hard implies effort which leads to work, then stress, then feeling bad, and ultimately shooting yourself in the foot.

Focus on what you already feel good about. Good feeling gives rise to gratitude, then satisfaction, then peace of mind, and ultimately more good feelings.

Each entry stands on its own, so you can open to any one page and reap the benefits therein. You might choose to read all eleven of them through once, then return to whichever ones speak to you in any given moment. So, allow yourself to experiment, be amazed, and be inspired! Most of all, enjoy them. Feel good!

It's All In The Words

Eliminate the words 'unbelievable' and 'incredible' from your vocabulary!

WHY?

Every time you use them, you deem whatever is being referred to as too dubious or improbable to believe, doubting its credibility.

How often do you use either of these words to describe something?

Think about it!

1- That movie was simply *unbelievable*. I couldn't take my eyes off the screen.
2- She demonstrated *incredible* skills during that tennis competition.
3- On my vacation, some of my experiences were truly *incredible*.
4- Shopping for a new car, I found the sticker prices to be *unbelievable*.
5- Looking back at my tumultuous upbringing, I can easily appreciate my *unbelievable* life now.
6- It was quite *incredible* to watch that trapeze artist fly across the air and catch the moving bar without falling.
7- Our students have such *unbelievable* excuses for not doing their homework.

If it happened or was experienced in some way...
IT IS believable!!!

Giving credit to life events with descriptors that are alive tells more about them and can feel a lot better!

1- That movie was simply *mesmerizing*. I couldn't take my eyes off the screen.
2- She demonstrated *spectacular* skills during that tennis competition.
3- On my vacation, some of my experiences were truly *awe-inspiring*.
4- Shopping for a new car, I found the sticker prices to be *ridiculous*.
5- Looking back at my tumultuous upbringing, I can easily appreciate my *blessed* life now.
6- It was quite *amazing* to watch that trapeze artist fly across the air and catch the moving bar without falling
7- Our students have such *lame* excuses for not doing their homework.

Let your Bright Spots be felt with emotions that are alive!

Bring power to your thoughts with purposeful words.

A Personal Challenge

The Challenge

Part 1- In the morning before you get out of bed, before you even open your eyes, list in your mind the things you are grateful for such as your pillow and bed, your pet, your breath, hot showers, a friend, and so on until you smile and perhaps experience a big aah!

Part 2- I invite you to find one good thing about each day and feel appreciation for it! It doesn't need to be anything monumental: things as simple as finding a close parking space, the book you dropped not landing on your toe, a call from a friend you haven't heard from in a while, a smile from a stranger in line at the grocery store, your coffee staying hot until the last drop, or your favorite song being on the radio as soon as you turned it on. There are as many things to be happy about as there are stars in the sky!

Part 3- Consider choosing a notebook or journal that suits you to list what you appreciated or what made you smile at the end of your day even if it was only one thing. You may also find that waking up with a desire for noticing something good in your day prompts you to actually create that "something."

The Results

You can count on your life becoming more and more extraordinary with each day that passes. You'll start to look forward to each day and what golden nugget you may discover in it. You'll feel good for no apparent reason. You may begin to realize that very few things can shake you when you have good feelings at your core. Even the inevitable days when things seem to be out of sorts will affect you less negatively because you will be aware of how you feel and remember to reach for a better feeling thought! Expecting good things will become habit. You will recognize in your own life, like you did through the pages of this book, that so many of us share similar kinds of dreams, similar kinds of things that give us joy, and similar challenges. Feeling a sense of oneness with the people around you and with the human race at large can be comforting, even exhilarating if you allow it. You can expect from this point forward to recognize the fluidity of every moment and a sense of calm and harmony, knowing that your life will never be the same.

"Mining the moment for something that feels good,
something to appreciate, something to savour, something
to take in, that's what your moments are about."

— ABRAHAM-HICKS

"You will never change your life until you change
something you do daily. The secret of your success is
found in your daily routines."

— JOHN C. MAXWELL

Tips for Getting You from So-So to Spectacular

Part 1-Affirmations – Repeating positive outcomes for your desires can be extremely beneficial. To enhance their effectiveness, write and/or state them in the present tense declaring them to be true NOW even if it feels "untrue" at first. Say them out loud with feelings of immense gratitude. Try standing up when you repeat them. Feeling grateful BEFORE a desire is actually manifested is where the power lies.

The prominent purpose of affirmations is to influence your thoughts. Even reading this book is a type of affirmation for you. I use affirmations daily. I repeat the same half dozen or so every day. Then, I add to my list as desires come up and delete the ones that have come to fruition. Keep it simple at first, then add more once you become accustomed to this practice. Do what feels good for you. Remember to truly feel each one as your current reality. Stating them by rote is no more beneficial than repeating the alphabet. Consider practicing with the affirmations on the opposite page related to feeling good, then create your own affirmations for whatever you desire.

Examples of my affirmations when I was looking for a house: "I live in a house close enough to the beach for me to ride my bike. I am thrilled with the open layout of my new house. There is a great deal of light in my house that my plants love." I did some visualizing as well. I saw myself approaching the bike rack on the boardwalk and felt the lock in my hands. I imagined being able to see all areas of the first floor from any given spot. In my mind's eye, I saw sunlight streaming in a window and felt the warmth of the sun. I practiced these visions and sensations every day until I found my house, which met those characteristics. It didn't happen overnight, but I continued trusting that it would at the perfect time. Simply doing these exercises daily lifted my spirits, keeping me motivated to increase my good feelings.

Sample statements to self:

1- Feeling good makes all the difference in the quality of my life.
2- I feel good through various means.
3- I love thinking uplifting thoughts.
4- There is a golden nugget in each experience I have.
5- I recognize what I am focused on in the moment.
6- I can tell how I am feeling at any point in time.
7- I have the power to shift my thoughts.
8- I am willing and able to do whatever it takes to feel good.
9- I choose to be happy just because I want to.
10- I choose joy and hopefulness regardless of my perceived difficulties.
11- I deserve to feel good about my life.
12- I prioritize my feelings of joy and appreciation.
13- I get a kick out of life.
14- I am a terrific person who shines on those around me.
15- Feeling good is my birthright.
16- I always have a choice in how I feel.
17- I feel good when I smile.
18- When I feel happy, I attract more reasons to be happy.
19- I see so many positives in my life.
20- I create the possibility of happiness for others by being happy myself.
21- All the good in my life comes to me because of my willingness to find happiness in each moment.

Part 2 - Empowering Questions – Checking in with yourself can be like looking at a map to see where you are now. Then you can decide where you want to go, how you'll get there, what you need to do to get there or what might be preventing you from getting there. Asking yourself quality questions can sometimes be compared to checking your temperature or checking where you are along your marathon route. Consistent checking-in can help you rid yourself of negative habits and limiting beliefs, and also increase your self-awareness. This process allows you to become more aware of your thoughts and habits. Once you become aware, you can make a choice to remain the same or shift gears.

Keep in mind that change is a process. Be sure to show compassion toward *you* if you fall short of the progress you had hoped for. There is no slip-up that is an actual set-back. Each moment holds the same opportunity to choose how you feel, regardless of what you chose in the last moment. Breathe deeply and appreciate your humanness.

Here are several questions related to the theme of this book: feeling good. Check in periodically during the day to determine where you are. If you're feeling good, express silent or audible appreciation. If you're not feeling so great, then reach for a feel-good thought to raise your spirits. You are also invited to come up with any questions regarding other topics that you feel might put you in a better place, guiding you to make a healthier decision or shift your mood. Get to know yourself! You *are* a pretty awesome person.

Sample questions to self:

1- What kinds of desirable and beautiful things am I experiencing in this moment?
2- Do I want to feel better and why?
3- Is there at least one good thing that has happened today?
4- Is there something good I can look forward to later today?
5- Do I like the way I feel right now?
6- What am I thankful for today?
7- Have I reminded myself today how amazing I am?
8- Have I experienced any successes today?
9- How will my life improve if I can be happy about at least one thing every day?
10- Can I build on just one happy thought until I feel great?
11- Can I focus on something good for at least 68 seconds continuously?
12- What dream can I dream today?
13- What does happiness mean to me?
14- What are the things that make me feel good when I'm doing them?
15- How often do I give myself permission to enjoy life?
16- Is there something I need to let go of to allow myself to feel good?
17- Am I willing to do what it takes to make feeling good a habit?
18- What routines or habits limit my feelings of absolute joy?
19- How often will I stop to check in on my feel-good level?
20- How often do I laugh just because it feels good?
21- How would I feel if I smiled most of the day?

Gratitude – The Game-Changer

111 Interesting Things That Can Make Your Life Extraordinary and That Feel Good

A –   amazement, apologies, art, answers, assistance
B –   blankets, books, bathrooms, bubbles, breath, beginnings
C –   camaraderie, courage, coffee, candles, choices
D –   dreams, dancing, dessert, donations
E –   enthusiasm, entertainment, emotions, electricity, encouragement
F –   friends, family, fun, forgiveness, flexibility
G –   green lights, goals, generosity, grass
H –   home, hugs, health, harmony
I –   intuition, integrity, ice cream, inspiration
J –   joy, jazz, justice, jobs, Jell-O
K –   knowledge, kids, kaleidoscopes, keys, kindness
L –   love, learning, lightning bugs, laughter
M –   music, memories, meals, mistakes
N –   naps, now, nature, nothing (Do we need a reason to feel grateful?)
O –   optimism, opportunities, oneness
P –   pride, projects, people, pets
Q –   questions, quietness, quality, quiche
R –   relaxation, refrigerators, rain, respect
S –   surprises, smiles, showers, sunshine, synchronicities
T –   trust, tolerance, technology, today, talent
U –   uniqueness, umbrellas, understanding
V –   visions, volunteerism, vacations, values, veggies
W –   water, weekends, walks, warmth, waking up, wisdom
X –   XOXO, Xeroxing, xenomania (the pleasure of meeting strangers)
Y –   YOURSELF
Z –   zippers, zoos, zeros, zeal

If you were to choose one item on this list and sit with the feelings of gratitude for it, actually saying, thank you repeatedly to yourself or aloud, you would lift yourself up immeasurably. Saying thank you and really meaning it can produce that feel-good experience that I've been demonstrating throughout this book. Expressing appreciation for just about anything can often bring immediate results. Feeling grateful has been known to reduce stress, anxiety, depression, worry, and frustration. Being in gratitude is our natural state. When you feel bad, you may wonder why you should say thank you for anything. It may seem senseless at first. Put those feelings into a deep sense of gratitude for just one aspect of your life, the air you breathe, and watch a powerful transformation occur. You may even feel tender emotion leading to some relief. It's certainly worth a try. If these concepts are relatively new to you, what do you have to lose? It will surely be a discovery you will be glad you didn't miss out on.

I'm certain that you can think of many more things you can appreciate in your life. I chose to list 111 examples. I like the number 111. It makes me feel good to write it and to see it. I'm not sure why, nor does it matter to me. It's just a fun number. Please add whatever things resonate with you.

"When you change the way you look at things, the things you look at change."

— DR. WAYNE DYER

The More You Look – The More You See

Exercise your feel-good "muscle."

It has been my experience that once I became aware of or began focusing on something, it started showing up all over the place. Let me share a few examples. After I had my first child, it seemed that everywhere I went, I saw babies that I hadn't noticed before. When I finally got the color car I really wanted, all sorts of vehicles the same color kept popping up. I decided it would be fun to find as many heart-shaped rocks or shells as I could on the beach. They appeared in droves.

In the first two examples, I would bet those babies and that color car had been there all along. I just hadn't noticed them because that wasn't where my focus was. In the third example, I had made an intention to find heart-shaped rocks and shells, so I kept that desire in my thoughts, seeing them in my mind's eye, and they became easy to see as I walked along the beach.

So, what does this have to do with your feel-good "muscle"? Everything. When you begin to intentionally look for things to be grateful for and/or simply feel good about, you will notice even more things that make you feel good. It's about your level of awareness. When you choose to experience a feel-good life, keep your focus on that outcome, and look for things that make you smile every day, you will surely achieve the results you desire. An important piece here is that you must feel what it would be like to already be living your feel-good life. Allow your emotions to amp up your desired outcome when you're thinking about them!

196

Key words:

- **Awareness** – recognizing what's going on in the moment, being conscious of your experience. Simply stated, "Notice what you're noticing."
- **Focus** – purposefully directing your attention or efforts toward a specific goal; central point.
- **Intention** – choosing an outcome; something to be brought about or created.
- **Amp up** – feeling more excitement; energizing your thoughts with emotion. Get fired up!

Exercises to increase awareness, both concrete and **abstract**:

Concrete- Find a picture with considerable detail. Look at it for 1 minute and turn it away from you. List as many items as you can remember. Then look at the same picture for three minutes and turn it away from you again. Your list of things you remember seeing in the picture will probably be longer. Chances are excellent that the longer you look, the more you will see and remember.

Abstract- Choose a day to notice how many times you get a good feeling about something. Do this for several consecutive days and you will most likely find more and more things to feel good or smile about with each passing day.

Balance and Gratitude

I tend to minimize the importance of things that aren't going smoothly simply because it's not worth giving much energy to them. When I do allow the rough spots to take the stage, I give them their moment in the spotlight, then as quickly as I can, I boot them off the stage and create a new scene with a better feeling character/thought!

However, I'm choosing to make mention of the foibles of one particular day to demonstrate a philosophy I aspire to live by and the value of that belief. There must be a balance in your world between the highs and the lows, and when you're able to recognize reasons to be grateful in any situation, you can create that balance. The balance then allows you to respond in a calmer, healthier, and more productive way.

Offsetting Challenges with Appreciation

Challenge - The cabin battery light in Van-Go turned red and was beeping leaving me with no refrigerator and no lights.
Appreciation - When I took her for a ride to see if the battery would recharge, it did.

Challenge - I went to the MVA to register the van and get a new license, but I didn't have my current registration with me.
Appreciation - I didn't get pulled over on the way.

Challenge - When I tried to start the van to leave, I heard a terrible noise and the notification said low fuel even though I had filled it up the night before.
Appreciation - It didn't breakdown in the middle of nowhere or when I was taking Megan to the train station earlier, it happened in the MVA lot in a safe commercial area.

Challenge - I called about roadside assistance and discovered that I didn't have it. I reached for my bank card to purchase it and I didn't have it. Once I did sign-up, it would take thirty-six to forty-eight hours for it to be effective.
Appreciation - My cell phone had a full charge on it, allowing me to make all the calls I needed to make.

Challenge - I didn't have a gas can so I had to walk about a half a mile to purchase one.
Appreciation – The sky was clear, my legs were strong, I had enough cash, and Target had one left.

Challenge - I walked to the gas station, got gas, put it in the tank but the van still made a strange sound when I turned the ignition, and it wouldn't start.
Appreciation - My daughter Rachel was able to leave work early and come pick me up, and the manager at the MVA office said I could leave my van there for a day or two as long as I updated them daily before they closed.

Challenge - I attempted to make two doctor's appointments while I was in town and neither of my previous doctors could fit me in before I planned to get back on the road.
Appreciation - I was able to find two new doctors that could fit me in.

I had faced enough challenges that day to have put me over the edge. In fact, years ago, they might have. I discover more each day that it is much easier and less wear and tear on my spirit to simply take a breath and look for appreciation somewhere in the "mess."

Know that there will be times when finding a better-feeling thought may elude you. "Don't throw the baby out with the bath water." Let it go and practice again the next time. No guilt. No shame. No throwing in the towel. None of that! Recall all those times when you *did* recognize the Bright Spots.

Be kind to *you*. Dismiss any derogatory thoughts or words about you. Pay close attention to your self-talk. It matters more than you can imagine. And if you ever entertain the notion of giving up on your new desire to choose feel-good thoughts, that is the perfect time to remember how amazing it feels when you allow yourself the pleasure of noticing one! You've got this!

Pathways - Choices

Every day, everywhere we go, there are decisions to be made: do this or that, buy this or that, say this or that, take this path or that and so on! How do we make the best choices? Most of the thousands of choices we all make each day are done in split seconds and unconsciously.

I was consistently reminded of this fact throughout my adventure on the open road. Obvious loud choices of where my next destination would be, how to get there, and when to eat presented themselves. I also faced the subtler quieter decisions. I recalled many hiking excursions where I had choices as to which path to take. Often, my choice was determined by how I felt standing before each juncture. Other times, the physical details, such as distance, ground condition, ambiance, my physical energy level, or even what kind of mood I was in, affected my decision.

Playing a little game with myself occasionally was all I needed to choose which walking or biking path to venture down. I would stand before the trailhead and not only imagine what might be at the end of the path, but what treasures or surprises might lie waiting for me as I progressed along the path. This process was especially fun when I didn't know much at all about the paths and when I could only see a short distance into the path before it began to twist and turn. I would wait for a gut response to assist me. Were they butterflies of anticipation or knots of trepidation in my belly? The former wasn't always the one I chose, but every choice, every path had its own merit and its own beauty. Examples of the wonderment of choice included skinned knees, getting lost, and swampy spots that sucked my boot off. On the flip side there were canopies of trees, birds chirping happy songs, dragonflies swarming around my head, deer, or other amazing creature sightings.

The gem that all the paths gifted me with wasn't always recognized in the moment but, nonetheless, was there, waiting for me to discover it! That, too, became a matter of choosing to see or not to see the value of my experience. I choose now as I did throughout my three-year journey across this expansive country, to seek out the gem in every situation. My track record is about 90%, but it didn't happen overnight.

Someone asked me once, why I would bother going through all that trouble instead of just resigning myself to the fact that some experiences are good and some are crappy and move on?

I told them, "because it feels good!" It actually feels great, knowing I have an inner guidance that helps me choose, and I love to play with it.

Van-Go Quotes

"Nothing is impossible, even the words say I'm possible."
—Audrey Hepburn

*"When you look at a field of dandelions, you can either
see 100 weeds or 100 wishes."*
—Author Unknown

"Laughter is timeless, imagination has no age, dreams are forever."
—Tinkerbell

"Never say never."   *"...just dance."*
—Author Unknown   —Anne Lamott

"Sometimes right in the middle of ordinary life, love gives you a fairytale."
—Hobbes (as in Calvin &)

"Laughter sparkles like a splash of water in sunlight."
—Charles Dickens

"Gratitude Rocks"   *"Oh, the Places You'll Go!"*
—Judi (Me)   —Dr. Seuss

"Take chances, take a lot of them. Because honestly, no matter where you end up and with whom, it always ends up just the way it should be. Your mistakes make you who you are. You learn and grow with each choice you make. Everything is worth it. Say how you feel, always. Be you, and be OK with it."

—AUTHOR UNKNOWN

"Every day holds the possibility of a miracle."

—ELIZABETH DAVID

"Whisper words of wisdom, let it be."

—THE BEATLES

"You're only given a little spark of madness. You mustn't lose it."

—ROBIN WILLIAMS

"It's not what you look at that matters, it's what you see."

—HENRY DAVID THOREAU

"If you want to fly, you have to give up the things that weigh you down."

—TONI MORRISON

A Special Secret To Improve Your Life Exponentially

Throughout this book, words and phrases such as feel-good thoughts, feeling great, happy thoughts, good news, Bright Spots, better-feeling thoughts are mentioned and advocated often. All these "concepts" have something powerful in common that I will reveal shortly.

When you recognize or reach for any thought that is positive, it allows an automatic sense of peace from deep within you to well up. You see, when that sense of peace is experienced, additional positive emotions lead to great-feeling thoughts. Feelings/emotions lead to thoughts. Those thoughts can then create emotions that lead to more positive thoughts and on and on, over and over. It is a very intriguing cycle! The fact that feeling good is beneficial to you in so many ways has already been established throughout this book.

Okay, so what's the big secret then? LOVE!

You may be asking yourself, "Love? What does that have to do with any of this?"

EVERYTHING

All positive emotions are love-based, meaning they come from a place of love. Love elicits all positive emotions, then thoughts and so on. Yes, love! Love is the essence of our true nature. You may be unaware of how valuable knowing that is to the ongoing quality of your life. Truth be told, every emotion, thought, action, and word you utter is either love-based or fear-based. The opposite of love is not actually hate. It is fear. Any negative emotion you feel can be traced to an element of fear. Fear is the "umbrella" under which all unpleasant feelings are found.

Where do you suppose all the Bright Spots came from? A place of love...unequivocally! Every single one of them! So, noticing how you feel in any given moment will let you know where that feeling is coming from. It will either be LOVE or FEAR. Love feels good. Fear…not so much. How do *you* want to feel? You can choose one or the other. Choosing a love-based thought not only amps up your state of being, but is advantageous to those around you.

Your job is to take care of how you feel, first and foremost. Some may say that is a selfish outlook. Well, maybe. Merriam-Webster alludes to the idea that being selfish is prioritizing your own needs and interests at the cost of others. I'm sure it can be interpreted as meaning that in some instances. In the case of seeing to it that you are in a good-feeling place where your emotions and thoughts are based on love as a priority…you are doing the most beneficial and caring thing you can do for you and for others as well. How do you feel when you are around someone who is in a very negative frame of mind? Probably not very good. I rest my case. Choose love when you feel a desire to shift your feelings. Choose love just because it feels better than fear. Living from a love-based perspective will never let you down. You just can't go wrong! Just imagine how your positive attitude, grateful heart and cheerful countenance could lighten the world you live in and shine on people around you. Go for it…choose love when you are checking in with your emotions each day.

On the following page, I have listed a good number of love-based emotions as well as several fear-based ones. So, you can better identify under which "umbrella" your feeling can be found! There are, of course, many more examples. These will get you started. Add additional words to either list if you feel it beneficial to creating a spectacular life! Awareness is key! It promotes choice!

Emotions

Love-based emotions: to be chosen and nurtured.

1- Happy	34- Colorful
2- Excited	35- Anticipated
3- Joyous	36- Appetizing
4- Alive	37- Magical
5- Thrilled	38- Loving
6- Blissful	39- Adorable
7- Amazed	40- Faithful
8- Delighted	41- Trusting
9- Vibrant	42- Amiable
10- Triumphant	43- Supportive
11- Energetic	44- Empowering
12- Light-hearted	45- Understanding
13- Bubbly	46- Courteous
14- Splendid	47- Compassionate
15- Interested	48- Sincere
16- Surprised	49- Generous
17- Motivated	50- Romantic
18- Terrific	51- Noble
19- Funny	52- Harmonious
20- Entertaining	53- Moral
21- Enthusiastic	54- Healthy
22- Captivated	55- Desirable
23- Curious	56- Gentle
24- Eager	57- Humble
25- Inquisitive	58- Tenacious
26- Astounded	59- Decisive
27- Touched	60- Brave
28- Intrigued	61- Adventurous
29- Impressed	62- Resilient
30- Fantastic	63- Patient
31- Influential	64- Passionate
32- Abundant	65- Successful
33- Refreshing	66- Attentive

67- Expressive
68- Intelligent
69- Willing
70- Active
71- Dynamic
72- Creative
73- Kind
74- Evolving
75- Teachable
76- Versatile
77- Discerning
78- Satisfied
79- Relaxed
80- Relieved
81- Serene
82- Grateful
83- Fulfilled
84- Introspective
85- Protected
86- Independent
87- Perceptive
88- Carefree
89- Worthy

90- Tolerant
91- Tranquil
92- Authentic
93- Mindful
94- Insightful
95- Understood
96- Present
97- Fortunate
98- Self-Reliant
99- Centered
100- Grounded
101- Free-Spirited
102- Peaceful
103- Ecstatic
104- Festive
105- Content
106- Invigorated
107- Capable
108- Influential
109- Confident
110- Observant
111- Truthful

Fear-based emotions: to be used as indicators for change.

1- Irritation
2- Depression
3- Blame
4- Powerlessness
5- Insecurity
6- Unworthiness
7- Guilt

8- Hatred
9- Pessimism
10- Revenge
11- Anger
12- Discouragement
13- Worry

What I Remember

Throughout my entire journey on the road driving across this vast country, questions were asked of me over and over again that I realized I didn't know the answers to. It made me doubt my memory and even worse, if I had been paying the least bit of attention. Questions like, "What did you see there?" "When did all that happen?" "Which body of water was that?" "How old was that theater?" "Which battle was fought there?" "How tall was that lighthouse?" "What was your favorite place?" My answers were always the same. "I don't remember. I really don't."

After much contemplation over a two-week period, this is what I concluded about what I remembered, and I was content with it. Those other details were moot.

- ❖ I felt inspired watching a rushing body of water completely surrender to gravity as it gloriously cascaded over the jagged cliff.
- ❖ I smelled the passing of time in the slats of the lattice covered bridge and heard the symphony of clopping horseshoes on the wooden floor planks.
- ❖ I felt the cool mist of the ocean on my face as the waves came crashing against the rocks and the salty water tickle my tongue.
- ❖ I heard faint voices in song seeping through the worn velvet curtains embracing the stage of an old theater and caught a whiff of a good cigar.
- ❖ I marveled over the workmanship of the sea-soaked fishing rig and wondered how many sunrises had warmed its hull.
- ❖ I imagined what loyalty and compassion that soldiers must have felt for each other. I felt saddened at how many young lives were lost. I felt my heart aching for the families who lost their loved ones to greed, anger, and fear.
- ❖ I meandered in awe through paths lined with trees and bushes of various species living peacefully side by side. I thanked them for their gifts of oxygen, shade, sustenance, and beauty.

- ❖ I noticed the music created by the dried autumn leaves beneath my hiking boots.
- ❖ I wondered just how a sailor, after many months at sea, must have felt to finally catch a glimpse of the rotating light that whispered, "You're almost home."
- ❖ I continued to feel how my life was being enriched by the people I met along the way. I felt their joy as if it were my own, saw their bright faces that made me smile, and relived the laughter we shared.
- ❖ I remembered the lightness and freedom that accompanies knowing happiness and joy each day.

Most profoundly however, what I experienced and remembered from my three-year journey across the country, and what this book is all about is:

- ❖ how recognizing a moment in my day that made me smile continues to enrich my life
- ❖ how we all have something to celebrate each day, though not everyone takes time to notice
- ❖ how many types of good news there are to notice each and every day
- ❖ how empowering it feels to choose to feel good
- ❖ how a single positive thought can supersede a hundred negative ones
- ❖ how a sense of gratitude can lift your spirits in a split second
- ❖ how connected it feels to share the gifts in your life with a perfect stranger

Those years on the road left indelible imprints on my heart and soul – imprints of gratitude, amazement, laughter, hard work, trust, surprises, self-inquiry, friendships, mishaps, fun, courage, patience, acceptance, love for life, and the opportunities that came my way. The undeniably magical experiences of sharing precious moments in the lives of so many people will live forever in my mind. I learned as much, if not more, about myself than I did anything else. I am humbled by it all.

Acknowledgements

I would be remiss in my recognition of those who supported me during the writing of this book if I didn't first express my heartfelt appreciation to two people in particular: my son Matthew and my husband Bob.

Matthew's support goes way back to 2008 when I published my first book, *Your Wish Is My Command*. He was an integral part of its entire creation. I owe the development of and the behind-the-scenes technical aspects of my websites to him as well. He insisted I have a travel blog when I went on the road, which ended up becoming the impetus for this book. For the love, time, creativity, objectivity, expertise, and laughter he offered from start to finish of *Journey Across the Smiles*, I thank him with all my heart. I could feel his passion for my intention and his desire to see it come to fruition whether we chatted on the phone or worked across the dining room table from each other. What a gift he is to me as a son, a friend, and a support system all rolled into one!

Bob's support began with the first seed I planted about writing a book. It continued through brainstorming ideas, holding down the fort during my marathon writing sessions (there were many), and telling me what a great job I was doing. The truly amazing contribution Bob made to this book was his suggestion for a title. After having considered dozens of others, as soon as I heard it, I knew it was the one. His explanation for the idea surprised and thrilled me. Viewing "journey" as a noun, it refers to my personal experience of what a privilege it was to be with people sharing their positive outlook and how good it felt for them and for me. Viewing "journey" as a verb, it refers to my invitation to you to spend your lives seeking out your own smiles. My heartfelt gratitude goes out to the love of my life for such insight.

I would also like to throw out big hugs of gratitude to my coach, Joan, who was kind enough to share edits previously missed as she read my pre-published manuscript, and my two writing buddies, Julie from Vancouver and Elizabeth from Australia! They shared my passion, my joy, my frustration, my laughter, and my tears while writing this book. With their unwavering support, it is here for all to read and enjoy! Thanks, team!

A Special Thank You to My New Mexico Family

While I lived there, occasionally my children would come to town from Maryland. I would orchestrate a gathering at a local restaurant so my New Mexico family could see them. There was always a great turnout to welcome and celebrate my beautiful children. After I went on the road and would return to New Mexico to visit, my loving friends would gather again at a restaurant to welcome me home, for however brief a period, and celebrate our delightful connection. Their hugs, loving words, stories of how life has been, and their very presence was more than I ever expected. They warmed my heart and let me know that no matter how long I was gone, there would always be friends to welcome me with open arms and grateful hearts. Having crossed each other's path in this life has left an indelible mark of love, friendship, and appreciation for them and for me.

Finally, I would like to mention my "High Vibes" kids. I started a small youth group when I moved to New Mexico. Three middle schoolers, Tiffany, Christopher, and Arianna were in one group and two elementary-aged brothers, Aiden and Liam were in the other. They were all on loan to me from dear friends. We met alternate Sundays getting to know more about each other and ourselves. The activities were designed to enhance their well-being in a variety of ways. It was a special time for them and certainly for me. I was able to see some of them when I visited New Mexico during my three years on the road. It always felt like I had never left. The only things different were a few added inches in height and some significant voice changes! I'm sure they know how much I love them, but I wanted to thank them here for having trusted me and welcomed me into their world.

Judi Ronco

About the Author

Judi Ronco lives her life with great fervor! She specializes in the upliftment of the human spirit and passionately guides others to seek the best in themselves and take risks that are likely to enrich the quality of their lives. What she teaches is what she herself has learned. She delights in her roles as an author, certified life coach, workshop facilitator, freelance photographer, retired special needs teacher, friend, sister, loving wife, proud parent of three adult children, and most recently beach-walker!

There were a couple of decades of her life when she was deeply and often negatively affected by the simplest disappointments. Drama seemed to spot her a mile away from a young age and latch onto her spirit like a leech, leaving her feeling helpless about her circumstances and hiding her sadness behind a well-crafted smile. Through trial and error, courses and books on self-empowerment, meditation, and the support of a few dear mentors, an ocean of tears, self-imposed victim mentality, and pure exhaustion began to dissolve into a spectacular adventure of self-discovery that continues to influence the positive trajectory of her life. A new woman willing to take responsibility for her thoughts, beliefs, feelings, and actions emerged and for the past 25 years, she has continued to become the grandest version of herself with each day. The smile you see today is blissfully authentic and she shares it unabashedly!

Judi loves to experiment with life outside the box. Her solo adventure traveling back and forth across the United States for over three years gives testimony to her desire to try new things in new ways. Simply inviting perfect strangers to share something good in their world and basking in their joy with them turned out to be a win-win surprise of feeling great for everyone involved. This led to a connection with people that she didn't anticipate, and became the driving force behind her book, ***Journey Across the Smiles.***

213

Judi Ronco

Wanna Do Me a Favor?

I'd love for you to take a few moments to post a review on
Amazon expressing what you enjoyed the most and what positive impact it
had on you, so that others may:

Be Open!

Be Aware!

Be Transformed!

Be Empowered!

and

BE HAPPY

as well.

I appreciate your feedback personally and as a writer.

Let me also express an enormous thank you for reading my book
Journey Across the Smiles!

Judi Ronco

Oh, just one last thought:

Joyous laughter is an audible

expression of gratitude.

Laugh a lot.

It feels soooo good!

Made in the USA
Middletown, DE
07 May 2021

38577651R00137